WHERE WAS "THERE"?

RE-EXPLORING THE BIBLICAL HISTORY OF JERUSALEM

David B. Carpenter

Printed in the United States of America

First Printing, 2019

ISBN: 9781091873278

ORDERING INFORMATION:

upspyre@gmail.com

Book Cover Design: Bobby Barnhill
Editing: Lakeview Publishing
Publishing: Lakeview Publishing
Cover Photograph: Angela Carpenter

Dedication

To my wife Angela

My companion on the trip to Israel,
And my companion on the journey of life.

CHAPTER INDEX

Introduction

I remember sitting in the church pew as a small child. It was somewhere in the midst of the tumultuous 1960's. I was old enough to know that the world outside the walls of our little Methodist congregation was changing, but not old enough to really be that concerned. My daddy would take care of us.

I recall when the only pastor I ever knew left our church when I was about 6 or 7 years old. He and his wife were getting a divorce. I remember his corpulent, red face as he raised his voice in the pulpit. He seemed angry. I didn't know why. I left that one up to my daddy, too.

Then there was the Sunday after Dr. Martin Luther King was assassinated. Our church organist played "Dixie" for a postlude. I don't think the pastor liked that. But my daddy didn't seem overly concerned. This too must pass.

Fast forward a half-century. My daddy died in 2016. He was 94. His generation was the World War II Generation. I am a Baby Boomer. In the decades since I was a boy, a lot of things have changed. In the 1960's, every television and radio station and every billboard screamed that the world was changing. Since September 11, 2001, it has changed more fundamentally, twice over. But this time, no one sent out a memo. Or an email. Or a text. Or whatever.

Thankfully, some things have not changed. I still believe what I learned, and in a sense, experienced in that little church more than a half century ago: that Jesus Christ is the Son of God. Something happened back there about 2,000 years ago that was so big, so earth-shattering, that even today we cannot deny it.

My childhood faith connected me with those events.

I learned that God wrote a book called the Bible. I still believe it and have found its' truths to be timeless, practical, reliable, and relevant today. I also learned that access to and fellowship with God is all about grace- nothing that we do, but what He has already done for us. The Christian life is about finding grace for ourselves, and extending that grace to others.

When I was a boy, there was a man in our church named Grover Sheffield. He had a beautiful, resonant bass voice. I recall him singing the song "Were You There?"

Were you there when they crucified my Lord?

Were you there when they crucified my Lord?

Oh! Sometimes it causes me to tremble, tremble, tremble,

Were you there when they crucified my Lord?[1]

Ironically, it was a song that is presumed to have been written by African-American slaves in the 1800s. It later became one of the first Negro Spirituals to be included in a major American Hymnal.[2]

I remember Grover Sheffield singing it in the days and weeks that led up to Easter every year.

---

[1] The Cokesbury Worship Hymnal
[2] Wikipedia https://en.wikipedia.org/wiki/Were_You_There

Those simple phrases and haunting chords compelled me as a child to live vicariously the story of the death and resurrection of Jesus Christ as we observed Holy Week all the way up to Easter Sunday, as the resurrection of Jesus Christ became even more real to me.

My maternal grandfather was a deacon at a Baptist church. He was a plumber from Washington County, Alabama and moved to the big city where the jobs were at Brookley Air Force Base during the depression and World War II. Later, in the 1960's, after he retired, and when times were more prosperous, he made a trip to the Holy Land. I still treasure the small marble statues he brought back from that trip a half-century ago. Today they reside in an honored place in my home office, surrounded by various mementoes, including some of my own treasures purchased in the Holy Land.

When my grandfather came back from the Holy Land in the 1960's, the latest technology was the carousel slide projector. "Granddaddy" (as I called him) was always an early innovator when it came to technology. His 1959 Chrysler was among the first cars with electric windows and factory-installed air conditioning.

Armed with his Kodak carousel slide projector, his 35-millimeter slides of the Holy Land, and a projector screen, Granddaddy hit the highways and backroads of southwest Alabama telling about the sights and sounds he had experienced in the Holy Land.

My favorite story he told was when they served him fish- in the Mediterranean tradition- with the head still attached. I remember him telling the crowd "When I saw that eye looking back at me, I decided I wasn't hungry." And that was unusual, because Granddaddy was always hungry as best as I could remember.

Fast forward ten years. I was a teenager. Our Methodist church had been through a couple of pastors, and a rugged man (with a glass eye) from Black, Alabama named Millard Spikes became our most recent. He was a sincere man with a real faith that even as a teenager I respected deeply. He invested in me and it was because of his influence I was called to the ministry, got my degree in Pastoral Theology, and have spent the majority of my productive adult years in pastoral ministry. In the 1970's, our church raised the money to send Millard to the Holy Land. No doubt when he returned, Kodak made another sale of a Carousel, and Millard shared his experiences to the delight of those who heard him.

I remember most clearly from more than forty years ago how profoundly the Holy Land changed him. He was a spiritual man before he went, but now he was a *deeply* spiritual man. He knew Jesus before he went. Now he seemed *connected* to Him. Somehow, walking those dusty roads and bustling streets transformed him in a way I could only imagine at the time. Even though honest tour guides will admit that practically all of the acclaimed sites in the Holy Land are not 100% for certain, some of them are pretty shaky, and others are downright disputed, somehow just being in the place where it all happened is a transforming experience, especially for the believer. It may have been right here, or right over there, or somewhere close by, but being there in those places is a life-changing experience.

I don't remember for sure which Carousel slide show it was on, but I recall seeing for the first time the picture of "Gordon's Calvary". Noting for myself the uncanny resemblance to a skull, I decided at the time that it must be on top of its' morbid summit that Jesus was crucified.

I could still hear the voice of Grover Sheffield echoing in my mind as he sang "Were You There?" I knew in my heart that one day I would go there to see for myself.

I also took to heart the challenge of the angel "Come and see the place where the Lord lay."[3]

I guess you'd say it got added to my bucket list, before the term "bucket list" was introduced to the lexicon. But I knew that one day I would personally go to the Holy Land and Jerusalem and see it with my own eyes.

In 2017, my wife and I were looking forward to celebrating our thirty-fifth wedding anniversary. We had been planning a trip to New York City. We had taken the kids to Washington DC a few years back when they were teenagers, and now they were all grown and busy with their own lives and activities, and this was the trip we wanted to take. September 11, 2001 was a watershed day for me, and I desperately wanted to see Ground Zero. I had flown over the Statue of Liberty and had seen it from the air. Of course, everyone wants to go to New York at least once, right?

---

[3] Matthew 28:6

But one day at a lunch meeting, some pastors again shared the story of their recent trip to the Holy Land, not with the outdated and extinct Carousel slide projector, but with a video projector and a PowerPoint presentation. This time the stars seemed to align. More precisely, the Holy Spirit began to speak. I knew if we did not go now, we might never go. The time was right, the funds were available, our health was good, and we decided to pull the trigger.

I was highly fortunate to take Bible History and Chronology in college from the esteemed Dr. Edward Reese, author of the *Reese Chronological Bible* and the *Chronological Encyclopedia of Christian Biographies*. Dr. Reese was known for having an amazing knowledge of the details of Christian biographies and history. The Chronological Bible was perhaps his greatest contribution to Biblical scholarship. I recently read on Facebook that someone had read it through in the last few days.

Somehow, it just never worked out for me to take Bible Geography and Customs, another of Dr. Reese's signature courses. There was always another course I had to take during that class hour. I was also intimidated by Dr. Reese's legendary attention to detail, which he expected his students to appreciate when taking his tests. (In all fairness, I did make all A's and one B in his other classes.) Anyway, up until then, my knowledge of Bible geography was more or less a patchwork, piecemeal amalgamation of places and names that had been assembled here and there, preparing for sermons, Sunday School lessons, and to teach college classes. My former associate pastor, Tony Ye had done a great series on places of the Bible a few years earlier, and my appetite was whetted.

So, several months before our departure date, I began to research and study about the geography of the Holy Land for myself. Truthfully, I probably did the work and study of a number of upper-level college or even graduate level courses on the subject. I began to put together an itinerary of places I wanted to see. So often I had heard that when you actually see these places, the Bible will come alive.

Someone made a facetious comment a few weeks before we were scheduled to leave that it looked like I was going to look for the Ark of the Covenant. I already had a reputation from a Vacation Bible School where I played the lead character in "Illinois Preacher and the Search for the Timeless Treasure." We spent all week uncovering a treasure chest full of golden Bibles.

Little did I know that what I would discover on my trip to Israel and the Holy Land, at least to my own satisfaction, was every bit as life-changing.

So, on the day before our thirty-fifth anniversary, we headed out for the trip of a lifetime. On this trip I learned some truly amazing things. On this trip, the Bible did more than come alive. As far as I was concerned, it was already a living book. But this time, the Bible began to correct my errant thinking.

Chapter 1
Touring Israel

Touring Israel and the Holy Land is not for the faint of heart. Most people who have a desire and interest to go don't get there until we are at least middle-aged. It's not an inexpensive trip, and international travel is a challenge to one's mind, body, and patience.

Thanks to our wonderful travel agent, Adrienne Tate, we planned to start our sojourn in Israel with a short stop in Tel Aviv to get over the jet lag and the long journey. After two delays, including a 24 hour wait in Philadelphia, and a layover in Germany, and an unexpected stopover in Turkey, we arrived more than a day late and totally exhausted. However, after a good night's sleep and a hearty Mediterranean breakfast, we were ready to go.

Based on my observation, the typical visit to the Holy Land has become a lot like 'Disneyland for American Christians.' Much of the time there, is spent on a bus and in hotels and Americanized restaurants with other Americans.

We decided against this approach. Instead, we hired our own Israeli tour guide, Dani Weiss, who is also an archaeologist by trade. We told him we wanted to see some things that other people may not always ask to see, and that we wanted to eat in the places where the locals eat. That meant we did not want our food or our experience to be 'Americanized' or toned down. He was more than delighted to comply with our request.

Dani also understood that we did not necessarily accept the claim of authenticity of all the sites that claimed to be genuine. He discussed with us the ones that have a strong claim to authenticity (like Simon Peter's house in Capernaum), as well as those that don't. Just because the house in Joppa says, *"House of Simon the Tanner"* (in English) doesn't make it authentic. We also had great discussions about Biblical terms and languages in their modern context.

When you visit Israel, it is not a vacation. Vacations are to rest, relax, and unwind. My visions of a few hours of touring and restful afternoons walking along the shores of Mediterranean were never to come anywhere close to becoming reality. When we got back, someone asked "How was your vacation?" I wanted to answer "I was on a pilgrimage. NOW I need a vacation!"

If you go, arrive in time to take a day to get over your jet lag. Then plan to be up early every day. Most hotels offer an Israeli/Mediterranean-style breakfast including eggs, cheeses, breads, fish, dried fruit and hummus. Several different types of salads are served at every meal. Fruits are available, and especially locally grown fruits like apricots and dates, in season. You can find bacon and pork in a few places, but they are rare. For the coffee aficionados, the coffee is good and strong. Coffee shops are available throughout the country for a mid-afternoon pickup.
Some hotels provide the evening meal as well, but for those that don't, there is a vibrant culture of independent restaurants that cater to every taste and are quite worthwhile to be experienced and enjoyed. When we were without our guide, we had no problem finding someone who spoke English anywhere we went in Israel.

Most of our days began before eight o'clock, with our guide Dani. (Most of the modern-day Jewish names are shortened versions of Biblical names: Dani is Daniel, Les is Eleazar, Avi is Abraham, and so on.)

We traveled and toured from seven-thirty or eight o'clock in the morning until about five in the evening. Many days we

* * *

walked five to six miles and some days more. Usually we did not stop for more than a snack and some expresso for lunch. By the time we were dropped off at our hotel around dinner time, we were very tired. After dinner, we would get in bed and read until about eight o'clock and then fall asleep, utterly exhausted.

A little practical advice for the Holy Land pilgrims: First, choose your traveling companion carefully. If you choose to go with your spouse, you need to have a strong, loving relationship. You will need to watch out for each other throughout the trip. Secondly, plan months ahead.

Buy lots of shoes, and when you think you've found the two most comfortable pairs of shoes you've ever owned, (and good socks are a must) and you're ready to start packing. My wife took a pair of sandals and found them comfortable.

● ● ●

Personally, I'm not a big sandal wearer.

It sounds like a cliché, but pack light. You're not going halfway around the world to show off your wardrobe or make a fashion statement. Choose items that match each other, because you never know what might be re-wearable. Plan to use the cleaners about halfway through your trip if you plan to stay ten days or more. My scheme for the trip was khaki, denim, blue and black.

Ladies will need to research what is acceptable at holy sites.

When I return to the Holy Land, I will purchase an appropriate hat, and not just a ball cap. I will also invest in quick-drying cargo pants.

After one night in Tel Aviv, and a stop in Nazareth, we spent two nights in Tiberias, on the Sea of Galilee. Galilee is a very peaceful and beautiful resort area. We were surprised how close Capernaum, the Mount of Beatitudes, "Tagba" (the location of the feeding of the five thousand), and Magdala (home of Mary Magdalene) all were in close proximity to each other. We ate fish caught in the Sea of Galilee, known as Saint Peter's fish- perhaps the long-lost offspring of the one my grandfather was offered fifty years ago. Gratefully, ours was delicious (and beheaded before it was prepared).

While in Israel, we toured Joppa (where Jonah ran from God and boarded a ship for Tarshish, and the house of Simon the Tanner from Acts 10), the Valley of Megiddo, Nazareth, the Valley of Elah (David and Goliath), Caesarea (where Paul appealed to Caesar) and Caesarea Philippi

• • •

(Matthew 16), and Ahab's summer palace (you might have heard of the famous sermon by R.G. Lee "Payday Someday"). We also took a boat ride on the Sea of Galilee and saw people of all nationalities being baptized in the Jordan River and heard them sing in languages we did not understand. However, their joy and devotion spoke volumes.

Jerusalem

We spent a little over a week in Jerusalem. The New City has grown up outside of the walls of the Old City. The Old City was a short walk from our hotel, and we went there practically every day we were in that area. With more than 3,000 years of history, it is one of the oldest continually inhabited cities in the world, if not the oldest. The problem with sifting through the history of Jerusalem is assembling all the pieces of that history- from the ancient Jebusites to the great kingdoms of the Golden Age of Israel, to the Divided Monarchy, the times of captivity, the era of Hellenization, the period of the Maccabees, the years of Roman domination, the years of Moslem control, the Crusades, and finally, the modern era.

Jerusalem is a complicated place, and its' history is more than a little muddied by the passing of time. As with other things, we tend to assume that they are true when they are not. Historical revisionism is nothing new. Usually history is 'modified' for a cause, a concealment, or just plain carelessness. Tradition is a powerful thing. See Mark 7:9.

● ● ●

The eras of Jerusalem's history basically occurred simultaneously with the Biblical account. There were, of course things that occurred outside the Biblical record. Following the fall of Jerusalem in 70 CE, the rise of Islam, the Crusades, and the modern era up to the Balfour Declaration and Israel's rebirth as a nation in 1948 makes the history of the nation look like the last play of a football game where the team that is behind 4 points has the ball and only a touchdown can win the game. They just keep lateralling the ball to whoever is standing until someone scores a touchdown.

After studying a multitude of maps both before, during, and after our pilgrimage, I think I am finally starting to get a handle on how the history of this city unfolded. Recent archaeological discoveries are shedding more light on this complex situation.

Chapter 2
The Final Authority

The final authority for understanding anything, including the history of Jerusalem, or anything or anywhere else for that matter is the Bible. The Bible has been proven undeniably accurate in every academic discipline, including history and geography.

Here is the problem: Once historians and academics think they have it right, they are highly resistant to change.

Aristotle lived more than three centuries before Christ. He was considered to be the greatest mind of his day. Aristotle postulated 'The heavier an object, the faster it will fall.' The academic community of his day had such great respect for him, and his theory made sense, so they all assumed he was right.

But he wasn't.

His theory would have been easy to prove or disprove. But it stood for 1900 years without being challenged. Then along came Galileo. He took two weights to the top of the

* * *

leaning Tower of Pisa. One weight weighed ten pounds, the other, one pound. He dropped them both simultaneously, and they both hit the ground at the same time. The heavier object did not fall faster than the lighter one.

The professors who saw the experiment still denied what they had seen. They just didn't want to admit they had been so wrong for so many years.

So, where was Jesus crucified, buried, and from whence did He rise from the grave? We do know and agree it was in or around the Old City of Jerusalem. We also know the cross and the empty tomb were close by and near each other. *"Now in the place where he was crucified there was a garden; and in the garden a new sepulchre, wherein was never man yet laid. There laid they Jesus therefore because of the Jews' preparation day; for the sepulchre was nigh at hand."*[4] But can we, with the benefit of time and the added perspective of modern archaeological discoveries be more specific than that?

We also acknowledge that just like any other city, the map has changed over time. In the case of Jerusalem, the confines (specifically, the walls) have been torn down and rebuilt a number of times. Keep in mind that Jerusalem has been invaded a dozen or more times, depending on

---

[4] John 19:42

who's keeping count. A small multitude of empires and cultures have dominated the city as well.

The Apostle Peter says, under the inspiration of the Holy Spirit says: *"We have also a more sure word of prophecy; whereunto ye do well that ye take heed, as unto a light that shineth in a dark place, until the day dawn, and the day star arise in your hearts: Knowing this first, that no prophecy of the scripture is of any private interpretation. For the prophecy came not in old time by the will of man: but holy men of God spake as they were moved by the Holy Ghost."*[5]

Any attorney, or judge for that matter, will tell you that a contract on paper, in black and white is more binding legally than a verbal agreement. This is the "more sure word of prophecy". The only way to know the correct history and geography of Jerusalem is from what the Bible tells us.

The facts as stated in the Holy Scriptures have been proven in the crucibles of time and experience. For this work, these facts, as given in the Word of God, will be the tent poles that support the overall structure that I will attempt to build. Reliable historical accounts will fill in between the poles.

While building on the Biblical account, I will attempt to use the methods of writer Jim Bishop. Bishop was a Twentieth Century author of several books, including *The Day Lincoln was Shot* and *The Day Christ Died.*

---

[5] 2 Peter 1:19-21

• • •

11

In the latter volume, Bishop takes the Biblical and traditional accounts of the Lord's last twenty-four hours and supplements the account with things that logically took place in the gaps where no account exists.

We shall take the whole counsel of the Bible narrative as fact. Then I will attempt to fill the void with reliable historical accounts. The Bible will create the foundation and the structure. Logic and reason will assist to fill in the details.

Chapter 3
Ancient Jerusalem

After the Israelites entered and conquered the Promised Land under Joshua in chapters 1-12, they realized that there were still cows to milk and bees to keep in the 'land flowing with milk and honey.' Cows are not always easy to milk. Anyone who has ever been slapped in the head with a cow's tail or had a half-filled milk bucket kicked over can vouch for this. Bees, likewise may raise "stinging" obstacles. The obstacles in the Land of Milk and Honey came in the form of heathen nations that still occupied the land after their initial conquests at Jericho and (eventually) Ai.

"And I will send an angel before thee; and I will drive out the Canaanite, the Amorite, and the Hittite, and the Perizzite, the Hivite, and the Jebusite..."[6]

Some four hundred years later, David conquers Jebus, a city that belonged to the Jebusites. That city has grown into what we now know as Jerusalem. Specifically, this area is known today as "The City of David."

• • •

To be clear, this is not the city of David's birth, which was Bethlehem, located approximately six miles South-Southeast of Jerusalem. Bethlehem was the city of David's *birth*. Jerusalem, the former Jebusite city, was his capital.

About 1050 BCE, David overcame the Jebusite forces and took the city. The Bible gives a clear account:

Then came all the tribes of Israel to David unto Hebron, and spake, saying, Behold, we are thy bone and thy flesh. Also in time past, when Saul was king over us, thou wast he that leddest out and broughtest in Israel: and the Lord said to thee, Thou shalt feed my people Israel, and thou shalt be a captain over Israel. So all the elders of Israel came to the king to Hebron; and king David made a league with them in Hebron before the Lord: and they anointed David king over Israel.

David was thirty years old when he began to reign, and he reigned forty years. In Hebron he reigned over Judah seven years and six months: and in Jerusalem he reigned thirty and three years over all Israel and Judah.

And the king and his men went to Jerusalem unto the Jebusites, the inhabitants of the land: which spake unto David, saying, Except thou take away the blind and the lame, thou shalt not come in hither: thinking, David cannot come in hither. Nevertheless David took the strong hold of Zion: the same is the city of David. And David said on that day, Whosoever getteth up to the gutter, and smiteth the Jebusites, and the lame and the blind, that are hated of David's soul, he shall be chief and captain. Wherefore they said, The blind and the lame shall not come into the house. So David dwelt in the fort, and called it the city of David. And David built round about from Millo and inward. And David went on, and grew great, and the Lord God of hosts was with him.[7]

Note these facts:
1. David was anointed King in Hebron at age 30.
2. Part of his time as King was in Hebron. The remainder was in Jerusalem.
3. David "took the stronghold of Zion". This is what is known as the City of David.
4. The Bible describes it as a "fort". It was about twelve acres in area.
5. Notice how the city was taken: "Whosoever getteth up to the **gutter**, and smiteth the Jebusites…" The Hebrew word translated "gutter" is *tsinnuwr*- a word only used one other place in the Bible. In Psalm 42:7 it is translated *"waterspouts"*. It conveys the idea of a conduit that conducts water. This fact will be key in later discussions.
6. Within this fort, there was a "Millo" or hill.
7. This stronghold, or city, became known as Zion, and was called the City of David.

---

[7] 2 Samuel 5:1-10

The Threshing floor

The Biblical History of Jerusalem begins with an understanding of the Threshing Floor of Ornan (or Araunah) the Jebusite in the city of Jebus.

Ornan was a Jebusite who owned a piece of property in the Jebusite city that was to become Jerusalem. This particular piece of property was a threshing floor, which offers a clue as to Ornan's livelihood. Although the Bible does not say, it is probable that he would have been a farmer, particularly one who grew grain. There is no doubt that Ornan and Araunah are the same individual, and it seems likely that *Ornan* (meaning "strong") was his Jebusite name. It seems his strength was political as well as financial, as he is identified as a prince[8]. Perhaps he was the leader of the Jebusite city. *Araunah* is a Hebrew name which means "Jehovah is strong." We could also postulate that this man came to know the Lord through the influence and testimony of King David and his followers.

We also find clues in the story of Ornan and David when the deed to the threshing floor is exchanged:

---

[8] *All the Men of the Bible by Herbert Lockyer, page 266*

Then the angel of the Lord commanded Gad to say to David, that David should go up, and set up an altar unto the Lord in the threshingfloor of Ornan the Jebusite. And David went up at the saying of Gad, which he spake in the name of the Lord. And Ornan turned back, and saw the angel; and his four sons with him hid themselves. Now Ornan was threshing wheat. And as David came to Ornan, Ornan looked and saw David, and went out of the threshingfloor, and bowed himself to David with his face to the ground. Then David said to Ornan, Grant me the place of this threshingfloor, that I may build an altar therein unto the Lord: thou shalt grant it me for the full price: that the plague may be stayed from the people. And Ornan said unto David, Take it to thee, and let my lord the king do that which is good in his eyes: lo, I give thee the oxen also for burnt offerings, and the threshing instruments for wood, and the wheat for the meat offering; I give it all. And king David said to Ornan, Nay; but I will verily buy it for the full price: for I will not take that which is thine for the Lord, nor offer burnt offerings without cost. So David gave to Ornan for the place six hundred shekels of gold by weight. And David built there an altar unto the Lord, and offered burnt offerings and peace offerings, and called upon the Lord; and he answered him from heaven by fire upon the altar of burnt offering.[9]

This threshing floor (in the fortress) was selected by the Lord God as the place where His altar would be set up. In order for the city to be defensible (which it was), it would have to be inside the city. However, it was rightfully and legally owned by Ornan. When David approached Ornan, and Ornan saw the angel, he bowed down to David, much like Saul on the Damascus Road, who having seen the light and heard the voice asked *"Who art thou, Lord?"*[10]

Ornan shows further respect for the red-headed king by offering to give him the threshing floor. This further establishes Ornan as a prince or king, as it was and remains the custom of earthly rulers to bestow generous gifts on one another.[11] David, however, wisely insists on paying for the piece of ground, thus giving the nation of Israel clear title to it for generations to come.

Now in order to fully visualize and comprehend this transaction, we must understand exactly *where* the city of the Jebusites was and *what* a threshing floor was, what it did, and how it functioned.

[9] I Chronicles 21:18-26
[10] Acts 9:5
[11] *The Scarlet Line in the Window.* A sermon by Charles H Spurgeon. (3168)

● ● ●

A threshing floor (see previous page photo) is a specially flattened outdoor surface used for the purpose of separating grain from chaff. There, the harvested grain would be thrown into the air above the threshing floor, where the wind would carry away the lightweight chaff and the heavier grain would fall back to the floor, where it would be gathered.[12]

With this, we now turn our mind's eye to the ancient Jebusite city now known as the City of David. This smaller city is located outside the modern walls of Jerusalem, south of the Dome of the Rock and the Al Aqsa Mosque, which are located directly north of the original city on the Haram esh Sharif, or "noble enclosure" otherwise mistakenly known today as the "Temple Mount."

The ancient Jebusite city was a crescent-shaped area, *south* of the (future) Haram or "Temple Mount". The threshing floor was located on the northern end of the city, south of where the Haram's retaining walls were yet to be built, likely on a Millo or hill which would be called the Ophel. To the north of the city in 1000 BCE was a singular, craggy mountain peak about fifty by fifty feet. This is the rock under the Dome of the Rock today. Three thousand years ago, it was difficult to access, and would NOT have been a reasonable location to take oxen and laborers to thresh wheat. It was not sufficiently flat, and it was isolated and likely too windy to thresh wheat.

Likely, had anyone even tried to thresh wheat there, both the wheat and the chaff would have been dispersed into the Kidron Valley below. This peak was later surrounded with retaining walls and filled in, and later still, further expanded. No one has been allowed to research its' contents for years. We shall also examine the probable historical identity of this area later in this thesis.

David gave God the best. He did not seek out a "high place"[13] like the craggy rock to the north, but instead dedicated to the Lord the best place to build his altar, and later his temple. The Tabernacle was four or five hundred years old. It had been transported and set up and taken down dozens of times. Undoubtedly, it was getting ragged, weak, and decrepit. Ancient Hebrew history tells us that many of the original items of the tent and structures had been repaired and replaced.

---

[12] Photo credit: Wikipedia   [13] Leviticus 26:30

It would seem obvious that after David sacrificed on the threshing floor, he set the Tabernacle up there. Now that Israel had their capital, they needed a place to worship. However, David understood that because he had been a man of war that he could not build the temple. This was left for his son, Solomon.

Now it came to pass, as David sat in his house, that David said to Nathan the prophet, Lo, I dwell in an house of cedars, but the ark of the covenant of the Lord remaineth under curtains. Then Nathan said unto David, Do all that is in thine heart; for God is with thee. And it came to pass the same night, that the word of God came to Nathan, saying, Go and tell David my servant, Thus saith the Lord, Thou shalt not build me an house to dwell in: For I have not dwelt in an house since the day that I brought up Israel unto this day; but have gone from tent to tent, and from one tabernacle to another. Wheresoever I have walked with all Israel, spake I a word to any of the judges of Israel, whom I commanded to feed my people, saying, Why have ye not built me an house of cedars? Now therefore thus shalt thou say unto my servant David, Thus saith the Lord of hosts, I took thee from the sheepcote, even from following the sheep, that thou shouldest be ruler over my people Israel: And I have been with thee whithersoever thou hast walked, and have cut off all thine enemies from before thee, and have made thee a name like the name of the great men that are in the earth. Also I will ordain a place for my people Israel, and will plant them, and they shall dwell in their place, and shall be moved no more; neither shall the children of wickedness waste them any more, as at the beginning, And since the time that I commanded judges to be over my people Israel. Moreover I will subdue all thine enemies. Furthermore I tell thee that the Lord will build thee an house. And it shall come to pass, when thy days be expired that thou must go to be with thy fathers, that I will raise up thy seed after thee, which shall be of thy sons; and I will establish his kingdom. He shall build me an house, and I will stablish his throne for ever. I will be his father, and he shall be my son: and I will not take my mercy away from him, as I took it from him that was before thee: But I will settle him in mine house and in my kingdom for ever: and his throne shall be established for evermore. According to all these words, and according to all this vision, so did Nathan speak unto David.[14]

Then David the king stood up upon his feet, and said, Hear me, my brethren, and my people: As for me, I had in mine heart to build an house of rest for the ark of the covenant of the Lord, and for the footstool of our God, and had made ready for the building: But God said unto me, Thou shalt not build an house for my name, because thou hast been a man of war, and hast shed blood.[15]

The time was coming for the building of a permanent place for God to meet with His people. The Tabernacle has served its purpose. The people of God are shifting from a nomadic lifestyle with a portable Tabernacle to a more urban lifestyle with a permanent Temple. The materials are being gathered. The man who God has prepared to build it has been selected. Even the Lord God has decreed it. The remaining question is WHERE will it be built?

---

[14] I Chronicles 17:1-15 [15] I Chronicles 28:2-3

• • •

Will it be built on the threshing floor that David purchased from Ornan where he sacrificed to the Lord, and where he reared the Tabernacle, or the craggy, inaccessible, indefensible peak some 300 yards to the north, outside the city?

Thinking of our perceptions of Jerusalem, one naturally thinks of the city as static and unchanging. But Jerusalem is a city that has been destroyed and rebuilt.

It is also a city that has been disputed for centuries.

On the next page is an illustration of the walls of Jerusalem. You can see that the boundaries of Jerusalem have been changed many times. As with many modern cities, the actual area where the city was founded is no longer the epicenter. Jerusalem has grown to the north and the west since the days of David and Solomon.

The modern walls (noted in green) are actually not so modern. For a reasonable fee, you can actually walk the ramparts of these walls, which we did during our pilgrimage. Warning, this is not for the faint of heart or out of shape! These walls were built by the Crusaders some 800 years ago.

The light blue and dark blue lines depict the location of the walls during the era when the Bible was written. These were the walls that Nehemiah rebuilt and the walls that Jesus prophesied would be destroyed, which happened in 70 CE.

The purple section is a set of retaining walls that were built around the fifty by fifty-foot peak of the mountain north of the original Jebusite city, outlined in red. During Jesus' time, this was known as the Lower City, while the more recent annexation to the west was called the Upper City.

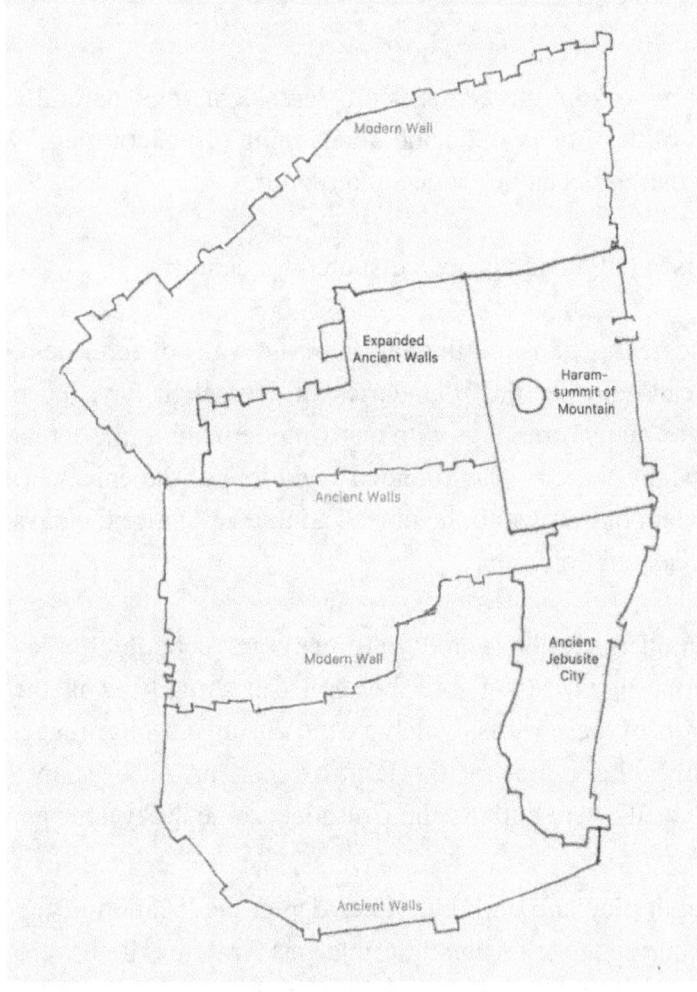

In maps showing the topography of Jerusalem, the Eastern Hill is the location of the original crescent-shaped Jebusite city, also known as Mount Zion.

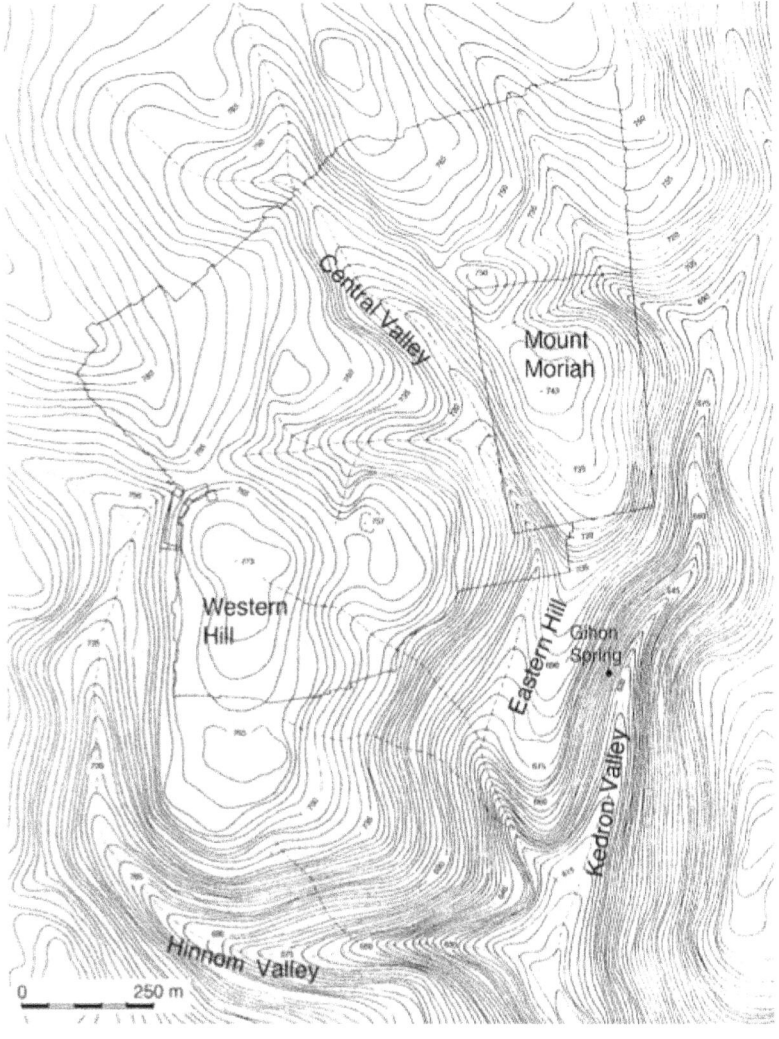

The Western Hill is the new Mount Zion, a subject that will be dealt with in a later section. The Central (Tyropoeon) Valley was mostly filled in during the era of the Maccabees, in the second century BCE.

Of particular note is the location of the Gihon Spring. It is the location of the gutter, waterspout, or conduit used to conquer the original Jebusite city, where the Threshing floor of Ornan was located, and where the Temple was to be built.

Chapter 4
The First Temple

The first temple, which is also commonly known as Solomon's Temple was built by Solomon in approximately 957 BCE. Like its' predecessor, the Tabernacle, it was in existence for about 400 years. The correct geographical location of this Temple is crucial to an understanding of the History of Jerusalem and where Jesus was crucified, buried, and arose from the dead. It is also crucial to correctly understanding eschatology.

There is no reason, other than tradition, that would locate this Temple, or any Temple on what is currently known today as the "Temple Mount", Mount Moriah, or the Haram.

This temple was built under the vision and guidance of Solomon, said to be the wisest man who ever lived apart from the Lord Jesus Christ Himself. It was so magnificent, along with Solomon's Palace and entire kingdom, that when the visiting head of state the Queen of Sheba came to see it, she said *"Howbeit I believed not the words, until I came, and mine eyes had seen it: and, behold, the half was not told me:"*[16]

* * *

This Temple was not only the meeting place of God and man, chosen by God, but it was the epicenter for all spiritual activity in Israel. It was there that the ceremonial sacrifices were made. These sacrifices were of paramount importance to the Jews, as they were a symbol of the coming Messiah.

Solomon's Temple was noted for its beauty and splendor. Its' exterior was beautiful, almost beyond description. But perhaps its' contents were even more amazing. The holy objects from the Tabernacle were obviously more durable and in better condition than the Tabernacle curtains, coverings, and other structural materials. The outstanding difference that sets Solomon's Temple apart from the others is the fact that it had the Ark of the Covenant. This we know because David brought the Ark into the city in a show of great triumph and celebration.

So David went and brought up the ark of God from the house of Obededom into the city of David with gladness. And it was so, that when they that bare the ark of the Lord had gone six paces, he sacrificed oxen and fatlings. And David danced before the Lord with all his might; and David was girded with a linen ephod. So David and all the house of Israel brought up the ark of the Lord with shouting, and with the sound of the trumpet. And as the ark of the Lord came into the city of David, Michal Saul's daughter looked through a window, and saw king David leaping and dancing before the Lord; and she despised him in her heart.

---

[16] I Kings 10:7

And they brought in the ark of the Lord, and set it in his place, in the midst of the tabernacle that David had pitched for it: and David offered burnt offerings and peace offerings before the Lord.[17]

Apparently, there was such celebration that Michal, the daughter of David's predecessor, Saul (and David's wife) criticized him for having disgraced himself.[18] Obviously, the Lord was not pleased with her attitude.

The ark had been stolen by the Philistines and eventually retrieved. Bringing the Ark to Jerusalem had been a reminder of the power of God's presence when Uzzah was killed as a result of transporting the ark on a cart, instead of being carried.

The Tabernacle had been, by definition, a temporary meeting place. A temple was the dwelling of deity. The difference between God's Temple and the temples of the heathen gods was the actual presence of God, who dwelled in His Temple. Specifically, He dwelt between the cherubim above the Mercy Seat on the Ark of the Covenant.

We should remember at this point that the original contents of the Ark of the Covenant had changed. Gone are Aaron's rod that budded and the container of Manna.

---

[17] 2 Samuel 6
[18] 2 Samuel 6:20-23

And king Solomon, and all the congregation of Israel, that were assembled unto him, were with him before the ark, sacrificing sheep and oxen, that could not be told nor numbered for multitude. And the priests brought in the ark of the covenant of the Lord unto his place, into the oracle of the house, to the most holy place, even under the wings of the cherubims. For the cherubims spread forth their two wings over the place of the ark, and the cherubims covered the ark and the staves thereof above. And they drew out the staves, that the ends of the staves were seen out in the holy place before the oracle, and they were not seen without: and there they are unto this day. There was nothing in the ark save the two tables of stone, which Moses put there at Horeb, when the Lord made a covenant with the children of Israel, when they came out of the land of Egypt. [19]

Despite Solomon's weaknesses and failings, he is still recognized as a symbol of wisdom and a great leader. The completion and dedication of the Temple is the highest hour of his life. It is a seminal moment in the history of Israel and Jerusalem.

And it came to pass, when the priests were come out of the holy place, that the cloud filled the house of the Lord, [20]

The Lord is pleased. Solomon prays a prayer of dedication.

---

[19] I Kings 8:5-9
[20] 1 Kings 8:10

Now when Solomon had made an end of praying, the fire came down from heaven, and consumed the burnt offering and the sacrifices; and the glory of the Lord filled the house. And the priests could not enter into the house of the Lord, because the glory of the Lord had filled the Lord's house. And when all the children of Israel saw how the fire came down, and the glory of the Lord upon the house, they bowed themselves with their faces to the ground upon the pavement, and worshipped, and praised the Lord, saying, For he is good; for his mercy endureth for ever.[21]

Understand here that under the leadership of Solomon, the people of Israel for as many times as they "got it wrong," this time they "got it right." When the Glory of the Lord fills the House of the Lord, God is saying "You got it right."

This means that not only the Temple was constructed right and set up right, but that the hearts that worshipped there that day were attuned to the one true God. And it also would mean that they constructed the Temple in the right place.

The First Temple Period

Solomon's Temple stood for nearly 400 years. Most historians date its' existence from 957 BCE to 586 BCE, (371 years to be exact) with the fall of Jerusalem. Solomon's death is usually placed around 931, or about 26 years after the Temple was completed.

---

[21] 2 Chronicles 7:1-3

Solomon's life is best understood by his writings. In his younger years, he wrote the Song of Solomon. The theme of this book is "Falling in Love with Jesus." In his middle years, when the Temple was built and dedicated, he wrote the book of Proverbs, reflecting his great wisdom.

Sadly, we see him as bitter and cynical in his final years through his words preserved for us in the book of Ecclesiastes. This downward spiral in the life of Israel's leader, Solomon, is also a reflection of the future direction of the kingdom. Everything rises and falls on leadership.

Solomon was the third and final king of Israel's golden age of the monarchy. It began with Saul, continued with David, and ended with Solomon. Each served forty years. Following this golden age was the era of the Divided Kingdom.

So when all Israel saw that the king hearkened not unto them, the people answered the king, saying, What portion have we in David? neither have we inheritance in the son of Jesse: to your tents, O Israel: now see to thine own house, David.
So Israel departed unto their tents. But as for the children of Israel which dwelt in the cities of Judah, Rehoboam reigned over them.[22]

---

[22] 1 Kings 12:16-17

• • •

The era of the divided kingdom began when Rehoboam became king and ten tribes withdrew and established the northern kingdom, Israel under Jeroboam. Rehoboam remained king of the southern kingdom, Judah. Both kingdoms eventually fell- the northern kingdom fell to Assyria after about two hundred years. Judah, the southern kingdom held on another 137 years and fell to Babylon. As was common in the history of the world in this time, when they fell the people were taken captive and enslaved.

During the First Temple Period, King Hezekiah came to power in Jerusalem. There were both good and evil monarchs during this period, and Hezekiah proved to be one of the best. He was a man of faith and prayer, who desired the best for the nation he had been entrusted to rule.

Now it came to pass in the third year of Hoshea son of Elah king of Israel, that Hezekiah the son of Ahaz king of Judah began to reign. Twenty and five years old was he when he began to reign; and he reigned twenty and nine years in Jerusalem. His mother's name also was Abi, the daughter of Zachariah. And he did that which was right in the sight of the Lord, according to all that David his father did.[23]

Up until the days of Hezekiah, the water for Jerusalem had been brought up from the Gihon Spring (in the Kidron Valley) through a shaft or conduit either discovered or expanded by the Jebusites. Again, this was how David had conquered the city.

---

[23] 2 Kings 18:1-3

And David said on that day, Whosoever getteth up to the gutter, and smiteth the Jebusites, and the lame and the blind, that are hated of David's soul, he shall be chief and captain.[24]
The word translated "gutter" in this passage is the same Hebrew word *tsinnuwr*, which means a hollow, or culvert. It is translated "waterspout" in Psalm 42:7, which gives some credence to the opinion that this "gutter" or conduit may have brought water all the way up to the city at times.

This access to water was imperative in making Jerusalem habitable, as it was the only supply of fresh water within many miles. The shaft made water available even if the city was under siege.

Hezekiah had the wisdom and foresight to expand the shaft into a tunnel. It has been uncovered by recent archaeological digs. I have been there and seen it for myself. On its' south side is the pool of Siloam, which was used for a ritual bath for those planning to go to the Temple. It was unquestionable for Temple visitors to cleanse themselves at Siloam, then traverse hundreds of yards to the Haram.

In 586 BCE, Jerusalem fell to Nebuchadnezzar. He burned the Temple and ransacked Jerusalem. About this time, between 624 and 587 was the last time the Ark of the Covenant was in the possession of the nation of Israel.

A myriad of theories exists as to the current location of this valuable piece of furniture, containing the tables of stone written by the handwriting of Almighty God.

---

[24] 2 Samuel 5:8

• • •

However, the only Biblical clue we have as to their whereabouts is in the Book of Revelation:

And the temple of God was opened in heaven, and there was seen in his temple the ark of his testament: and there were lightnings, and voices, and thunderings, and an earthquake, and great hail.[25]

At the beginning of the First Temple Period, the people of Israel had great leaders, prosperity, a new capital, progress, freedom, the Ark of the Covenant, and the presence of God in the house of God. During these years, things went terribly wrong and by the end of this era, it seems they lost it all because they took it all for granted.

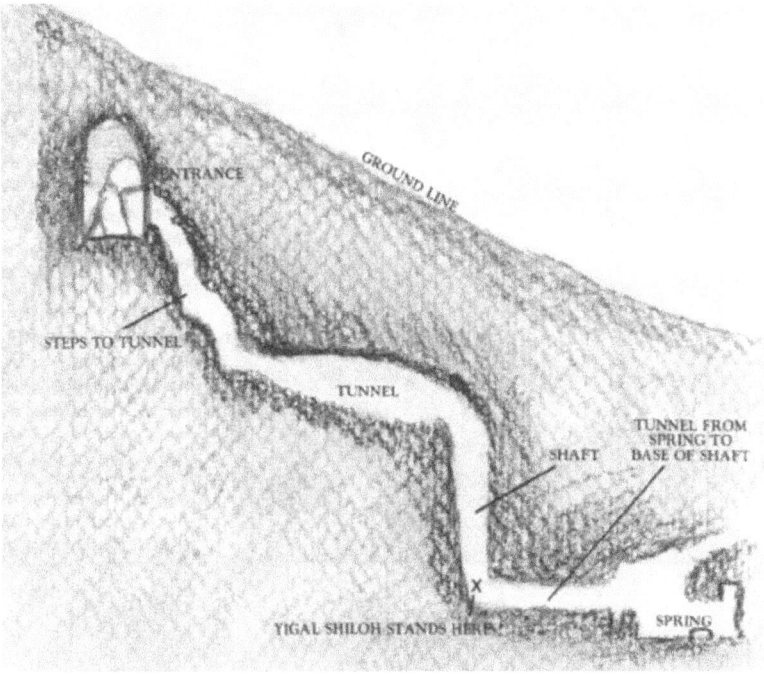

---

[25] Revelation 11:1

• • •

Note the location of the Gihon Spring, which is in the City of David, not under the Haram.

Chapter 5
The Second Temple

Fifty years after the fall of Jerusalem and destruction of Solomon's Temple, work was started on a second temple in 536 BCE. It was built on the ruins of the First Temple. This fact establishes that it was built on the same location. This structure would be known as Zerubbabel's Temple, and later restored as Herod's Temple. Again, after only fifty years, it is certain that the location of the previous temple was obvious, and that the second temple was built on the same site.

This reconstruction began with Ezra, a scribe knowledgeable of the law of Moses. He secured permission from the king of Persia to reestablish the nation of Israel. The king gave the decree, and the Jews were free to return to their ancestral homeland.

They were also allowed to carry valuables and precious metals with them to offer to the Lord. Since the wealth of the temple had been raided a generation ago, and the Ark of the Covenant had disappeared, it would be necessary for the Jews to attain such materials in order to build a new

• • •

temple.[26]

Once the people arrived, again apathy and lethargy began to set in. Haggai the prophet gave a stout warning:

In the second year of Darius the king, in the sixth month, in the first day of the month, came the word of Jehovah by Haggai the prophet unto Zerubbabel the son of Shealtiel, governor of Judah, and to Joshua the son of Jehozadak, the high priest, saying, Thus speaketh Jehovah of hosts, saying, This people say, It is not the time for us to come, the time for Jehovah's house to be built. Then came the word of Jehovah by Haggai the prophet, saying, Is it a time for you yourselves to dwell in your ceiled houses, while this house lieth waste?[27]

In the seventh month, in the one and twentieth day of the month, came the word of the Lord by the prophet Haggai, saying, Speak now to Zerubbabel the son of Shealtiel, governor of Judah, and to Joshua the son of Josedech, the high priest, and to the residue of the people, saying, Who is left among you that saw this house in her first glory? and how do ye see it now? is it not in your eyes in comparison of it as nothing? Yet now be strong, O Zerubbabel, saith the Lord; and be strong, O Joshua, son of Josedech, the high priest; and be strong, all ye people of the land, saith the Lord, and work: for I am with you, saith the Lord of hosts: According to the word that I covenanted with you when ye came out of Egypt, so my spirit remaineth among you: fear ye not.

---

[26] *Annals of the World,* by James Ussher

[27] Haggai 1:1-4

• • •

For thus saith the Lord of hosts; Yet once, it is a little while,
and I will shake the heavens, and the earth, and the sea, and
the dry land;
And I will shake all nations, and the desire of all nations
shall come: and I will fill this house with glory, saith the
Lord of hosts.
The silver is mine, and the gold is mine, saith the Lord of hosts.
The glory of this latter house shall be greater than of the
former, saith the Lord of hosts: and in this place will I
give peace, saith the Lord of hosts.[28]

This reminder that "The silver is mine, and the gold is mine…" is perhaps an indication that the people who had transported those materials back to Jerusalem had decided to keep a percentage as a "finder's fee" to start their own financial empire or even outright had misappropriated it.

Apparently, however, the fact that these metals were used in the temple also speaks to the fact that they were not as abundant as the materials that had been gathered by Solomon. Zerubbabel's temple, though larger in size, ended up being far less in opulence.

A second decree went out from Darius and the process of building the temple was reignited. It was completed soon thereafter.

---

[28] Haggai 2:1-9

Then Darius the king made a decree, and search was made in the house of the archives, where the treasures were laid up in Babylon. And there was found at Achmetha, in the palace that is in the province of Media, a roll, and therein was thus written for a record: In the first year of Cyrus the king, Cyrus the king made a decree: Concerning the house of God at Jerusalem, let the house be builded, the place where they offer sacrifices, and let the foundations thereof be strongly laid; the height thereof threescore cubits, and the breadth thereof threescore cubits; with three courses of great stones, and a course of new timber: and let the expenses be given out of the king's house. And also let the gold and silver vessels of the house of God, which Nebuchadnezzar took forth out of the temple which is at Jerusalem, and brought unto Babylon, be restored, and brought again unto the temple which is at Jerusalem, every one to its place; and thou shalt put them in the house of God. Now therefore, Tattenai, governor beyond the River, Shethar-bozenai, and your companions the Apharsachites, who are beyond the River, be ye far from thence: let the work of this house of God alone; let the governor of the Jews and the elders of the Jews build this house of God in its place.[29]

Ezra also records a key reaction to the new temple by the people. Again, it demonstrates that although this second temple might have had a larger footprint than the first, it lacked much in splendor and beauty.

---

[29] Ezra 6:1-7

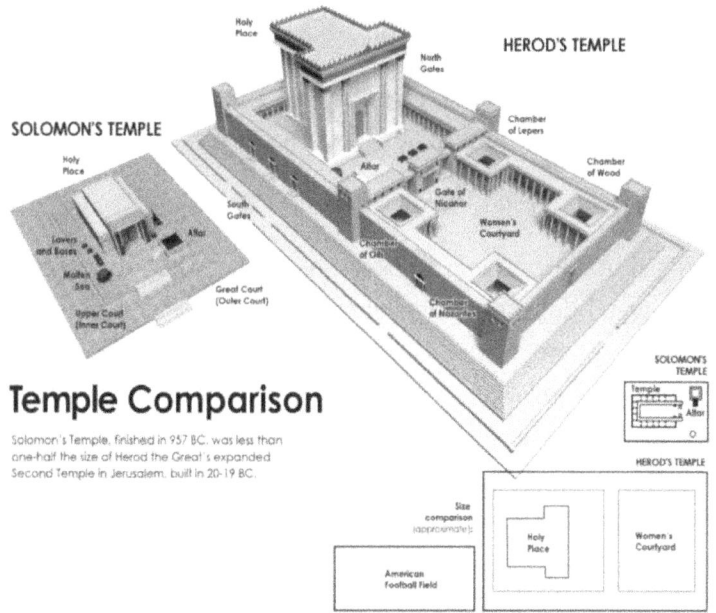

Temple Comparison

SOLOMON'S TEMPLE

HEROD'S TEMPLE

Solomon's Temple, finished in 957 BC, was less than one-half the size of Herod the Great's expanded Second Temple in Jerusalem, built in 20-19 BC.

And they sang together by course in praising and giving thanks unto the Lord; because he is good, for his mercy endureth for ever toward Israel. And all the people shouted with a great shout, when they praised the Lord, because the foundation of the house of the Lord was laid. But many of the priests and Levites and chief of the fathers, who were ancient men, that had seen the first house, when the foundation of this house was laid before their eyes, wept with a loud voice; and many shouted aloud for joy: So that the people could not discern the noise of the shout of joy from the noise of the weeping of the people: for the people shouted with a loud shout, and the noise was heard afar off.[30]

---

[30] Ezra 3:11-13

The old men, who had seen the majesty of Solomon's Temple could not be joyful over the second temple. The young men, who had lived much of their lives without a temple, were just grateful to have one. Again we see that tradition is a powerful force.

Again, it is important to note, however, that the second temple was built only fifty years after the destruction of the first one. There were people who were alive to see both temples. As a matter of fact, they objected to some things about the new temple, because they were able to compare it to the former one. But notice that there was no objection to the <u>location</u> of the new temple, because it was built on the same spot as the old one.

Even to this day, the Jews pray at the Western Wall, because they believe it is the place closest to where the Holy of Holies was. Orthodox Jews will not go on the Temple Mount because they do not want to walk across the place where (they believe) the Holy of Holies was, even they do not claim to know exactly where that spot might have been. With this in mind, how can we believe that these Jews in Ezra's day would not have heartily objected to the Temple being relocated from the original site at the threshing floor of Ornan the Jebusite in the City of David? The obvious answer is that they would have objected, and therefore, the second Temple was on the same site as the first- above the Gihon Springs, in the original Jebusite city known today as the City of David.

The temple is dedicated in 515, and a few years later, Artaxerxes releases Nehemiah to return to Jerusalem to secure it by rebuilding the walls. The job is completed. In

● ● ●

less than fifty years, Malachi writes the closing words to the Old Testament.

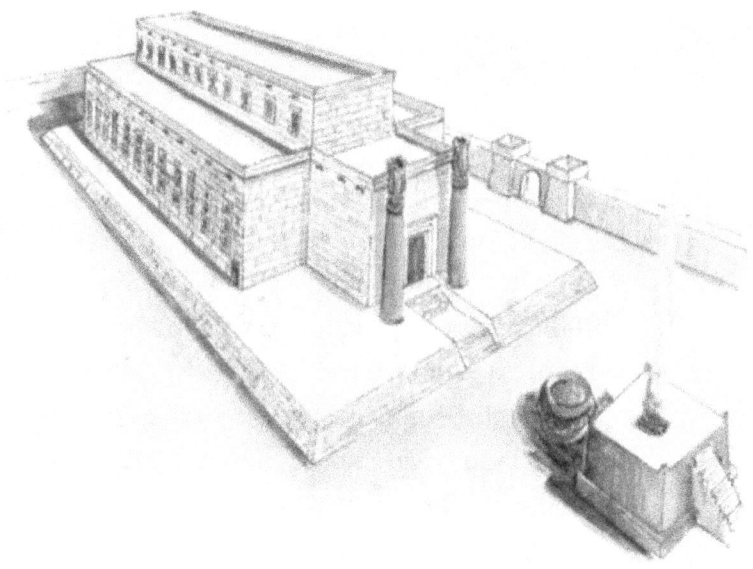

REVIEW OF THE TEMPLE IN THE OLD TESTAMENT PERIOD

1. David purchases the Threshing Floor from Araunah (2 Samuel 24:21). This took place in 1017 BCE.

2. Solomon builds the First Temple on that same Threshing Floor, approximately fifty years later. *"Then Solomon began to build the house of the Lord at Jerusalem in mount Moriah, where the Lord appeared unto David his father, in the place that David had prepared in the threshingfloor of Ornan the Jebusite."*[31]

3. Note that the Temple was constructed *in the place* that was prepared- the Threshingfloor of Ornan the Jebusite, in the **original** Jebusite city or fortress.

4. The Temple is dedicated in 2 Chronicles 6.

5. By 700 BCE, construction was underway (by Hezekiah) to connect the Temple Mount to the water from the Gihon Spring. This would be called a gutter, conduit, waterspout, or tunnel. Nehemiah also mentions a brook (2:15) and a river (3:7), some 250 years later.

6. In 586 BCE, Jerusalem fell, and Solomon's Temple was destroyed.

7. It was rebuilt in 535. This was known as Zerubbabel's Temple.

8. This Temple was refurbished by Herod, and subsequently became known as Herod's Temple, which was the Temple in Jesus' time.

---

[31] 2 Chronicles 3:1

• • •

Chapter 6
The Inter-Testamental Period

The Inter-Testamental period is naturally defined as the time from the chronological last phrase of the Old Testament until the first phrase of the New Testament. Most scholars attribute Malachi's final prophecy at around 397 BCE. Likewise, the annunciation of the angel Gabriel to Mary and Elisabeth and the birth of Jesus around 4 BCE. Many people are not aware of the historical developments that took place in Jerusalem during this 400-year period.

This was all a part of the Second Temple Period. This second temple will remain standing for about 500 years, until 70 CE.

During the intertestamental period, life in Jerusalem was not without its changes. These changes were both global and local. Truly, change is the only constant.

This period begins with the passing of Ezra, Nehemiah, and Malachi. Ezra and Nehemiah were looked to as great

• • •

leaders, and though we know little of Malachi the man, it was said by his contemporaries that he was suspected of being an angel incarnate.[32]   Along with these luminaries were those who survived captivity and saw both temples. With their passing, the stage was set for a new era of change.

Around the middle of the fourth century BCE, 356 to be exact, a young royal was born in Pella, in the Greek kingdom of Macedon. He was named Alexander. He would succeed his father Philip II to the throne at the age of twenty. His brief thirteen-year reign ended with his final lament that "There are no more worlds to conquer."[33]

Alexander the Great did indeed conquer worlds. It has been said that he never lost a battle. The territories he conquered covered a large percentage of the then-civilized world. His empire extended from Greece into most of modern-day Egypt and westward to India.

His territorial conquest more than swallowed up the Egyptian and Babylonian empires and even added to the expansive Achaemind, or Medo-Persian empire.

Alexander conquered not only through military might, but through the spread of Greek ideology. This Hellenization or spread of Greek culture eventually made its' way to Jerusalem.

---

[32] *All the Men of the Bible*
by Herbert Lockyer,
Zondervan 1968

[33] Wikiquote

• • •

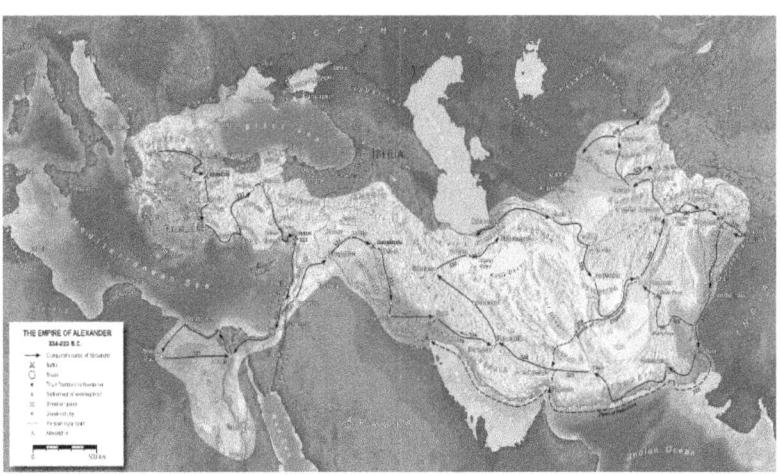

So, in 334 BCE, Alexander's spread of Hellenism began in the near East. In 332, as he approached Jerusalem, the high priest had a dream. He instructed the people to dress in white garments, and the priests to wear their priestly clothing. As Alexander and his armies approached, they processed outside the city walls. Alexander stopped, dismounted, and approached them on foot. His soldiers, expecting to attack, were in disbelief. Alexander explained that he had seen the high priest in a dream. Alexander was received into the city, the city was spared, and the Jews were allowed to continue to enjoy the laws of their forefathers.[34] Hellenism and Greek culture were on a path toward full acceptance in Jerusalem.

In 323, Alexander died. His kingdom was divided amongst his four generals. Jerusalem, Israel, and parts west fell under the Seleucid Dynasty. The assimilation of a Hellenistic philosophy and lifestyle continued.

---

[34] *Antiquities of the Jews* by Flavius Josephus. Book 11, Chapter 8, paragraphs 4 and 5.

Word traveled slowly in ancient times. Things changed slowly, but they changed. In 169, a scant 154 years after the death of Alexander, Antiochus Epiphanes came to power in Jerusalem. In a relatively short time, he banned circumcision and the observance of the Sabbath. This enraged the older, more orthodox Jews, but was embraced by the younger generation, who began to intermarry with Gentiles. He even constructed a sports stadium in Jerusalem.[35]

Then things went from bad to worse. He raided the temple of all its' valuables. Then to add insult to injury, he sacrificed a pig (an unclean animal) on the altar, thus defiling the temple and the holy place itself.

A priest named Mattathias the Hasmonean saw what was happening around him. He knew that it was time to take action or see his people perish. Mattathias had five sons. Upon his death, his son Judah Maccabee (who is best remembered for initiating Hanukkah) took over his father's somewhat unofficial leadership position.

While Antiochus was attempting to expand his empire in Egypt, a rumor spread that he had been killed. The deposed high priest gathered a group of soldiers and attacked Jerusalem. When Antiochus returned from Egypt and realizing what had happened, attacked Jerusalem and executed many Jews.

---

[35] 1 Maccabees 1:14

● ● ●

Some sources say that Antiochus himself died while on an expedition in 164 of an illness that may have been either physical or mental.[36]

Meanwhile, the Hasmonean Dynasty began the second of only three times that the Jews would autonomously rule their own land, with the other two being under the pre-divided monarchy and the other being the present time. The temple was cleansed, and worship was restored. Hellenism was defeated.

One of the most interesting figures in the Hasmonean period was Simon the Hasmonean. Apparently, between the years of 142 and 134, he led in the truncation of Mount Zion, moving massive amounts of dirt and rocks from the southeast ridge to fill in the Central Valley and build up the southwest ridge. Amazingly, this was done in a period of three years by three thousand men, one bucket at a time. As the inter-testamental period draws to a close, we have begun to see the formations for the Jerusalem that Jesus knew. It has changed geographically, expanding even further to the west now that the new Mount Zion on the southwest ridge had been built up.

Once more, however, trouble comes to the Holy City, this time in the form of the burgeoning Roman Empire, which is taking over the territory of the Seleucids and the Greeks.

---

[36] *Israel Exploration Journal*, Doron Mendels, Vol. 31, No. 1/2 (1981), pp. 53-56

In 63 the Roman General Pompey captures Jerusalem. This sets the scene for a series of Roman Governors.

Of note is Herod the Great, who comes to power in 37 BCE and reigned until his death 33 years later in 4 BCE.

Herod was raised a Jew. Apparently, the Romans thought that he would understand the Jews and that they would accept him. However, his responsibility for the murder of the innocents leaves his hands dripping with the blood of a multitude of Jewish infants.

Herod was a builder. He was responsible for building the Mediterranean resort of Caesarea, the mountain retreat at Masada near the Dead Sea, Fortress Antonia, and for restoring the Temple in Jerusalem. Of course, he built himself a palace on the western side of the city. In addition, his various public works projects included an aqueduct system as well as underground sewers. He also rebuilt the weakened sections of the city walls.

Please note that the first Temple was built above the Gihon Spring, on the former threshing floor of Ornan the Jebusite, in the City of David. The second temple was built on the same site. There is no reason to believe that at any time the temple was moved to the present site of the Dome of the Rock.

Chapter 7
Thirty-Six Acres

So we turn our attention from the history that proves that the Temple was located in the city of David to the geography of a massive set of retaining walls being built around a rocky mountain peak north of the Temple, which is erroneously known in our day as the "Temple Mount."

Where did it come from, and what was its' original purpose?

One idea might come from subterranean structures that might indicate that the southern end of the structure was originally used for Solomon's stables. Undoubtedly, when enemy forces overran Jerusalem and destroyed the Temple, they still needed places to stable their horses.

Likely, if part of this thirty-six acre complex was originally Solomon's stables, it would make sense. While some archaeologists have theorized that it is not solid earth, but rather is compartmentalized, no one with substantial proof has submitted it for honest review.

Again, we know that Herod the Great was a great builder. Based on his record of other building projects, it is not

• • •

difficult to assume that he could have refurbished and enlarged this area, but again, for what purpose?

This question leads us to another question: Where was the location of Fortress Antonia? Herod loved to name things for his friends, and this one was named for Mark Antony. It was the headquarters of the Tenth Roman Legion, which was stationed in Jerusalem.

The Tenth Roman Legion consisted of about 6,000 soldiers and another 4,000 support personnel. A typical Roman army camp required adequate food and water. Herod (the builder) constructed an aqueduct system that could have supplied water. Cooks were needed to prepare the food, medical personnel, pagan clergy for their temples, prostitutes, servants to at least help care for the horses and other needs-the Roman army camp was a massive operation.

Most historical records show Fortress Antonia as a rather small appendage on the northwest corner of the "Temple Mount." However, no historical evidence of its existence has ever been found on the northwest corner of the so-called Temple Mount, or for that matter, <u>anywhere else</u> <u>in ancient Jerusalem.</u>

So where was Fortress Antonia and what was this 36-acre site? Where was the Roman encampment? It is no coincidence that almost every Roman army camp excavated from this

• • •

time was approximately… 35 acres! This makes it obvious that the so-called "Temple Mount" was never the Temple Mount at all, but rather, the Roman army camp, Fortress Antonia.

There were cisterns for gathering the rare rainwater on the Haram. It is also possible that Herod's aqueduct supplied it with water. But the fresh running water required for washing was never under the Temple Mount, it was only available at the Gihon Springs, located south of the Temple Mount, in the City of David. This is where the Temple was located, not on the Temple Mount.

Here is an artist's conception of what it might have looked like. It shows the Temple located over the Gihon Spring, to the south of Fortress Antonia (the elevated platform to the north where the Dome of the Rock is located today).

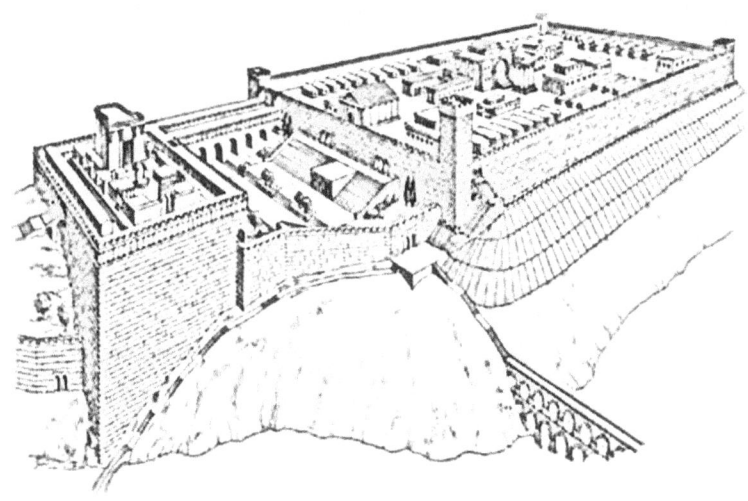

We walked through this area on foot while we were in Jerusalem. No one seems to be aware that this could have been the very location of the Temple of Israel.

What Saith the Scriptures?

And Jesus went out, and departed from the temple: and his disciples came to him for to shew him the buildings of the temple. And Jesus said unto them, See ye not all these things? verily I say unto you, There shall not be left here one stone upon another, that shall not be thrown down.[37]

---

[37] Matthew 24:1-2

In this passage, first notice that Jesus had just departed from the Temple. His disciples are showing Him the buildings of the temple. Then Jesus makes a stunning prophecy in reference to "all these things". He said that "There shall not be left here one stone upon another, that shall not be thrown down." A declarative statement, made by God in human flesh, quoted in the inerrant Word of God. Seems pretty clear cut.

So why are there stones still standing on what we have been told is the "Temple Mount"? The Muslims use this as an opportunity to point out that Jesus was not infallible.

Any archaeologist can point out the pre-Herodian stones and Herodian stones that are still in the wall of the Temple Mount until this very day. They were not thrown down when the Temple was destroyed, and the city was ransacked.

Jesus' prophecy was not the only one.

Micah the Morasthite prophesied in the days of Hezekiah king of Judah, and spake to all the people of Judah, saying, Thus saith the Lord of hosts; Zion shall be plowed like a field, and Jerusalem shall become heaps, *and the mountain of the house as the high places of a forest.*[38]

Notice the phrase *"Zion shall be plowed like a field…"* Zion, the Holy Mountain, the actual location of the Temple would be plowed like a field.

---

[38] Jeremiah 26:18

Here is a picture of the City of David made from the south sometime before the gold was applied to the Dome of the Rock, which began in 1959. Notice that the area of the original city of David is plowed for cultivating crops. The Haram, or Temple Mount is in the upper section of the picture, which means the picture is looking north. Visible in the foreground is the dome of the El Aqsa Mosque, which is also located on the Temple Mount. The crest of the Mount of Olives, located to the east, is visible in the upper right corner.

What Saith the Other Witnesses?

But if he will not hear thee, then take with thee one or two more, that in the mouth of two or three witnesses every word may be established.[39]

---

[39] Matthew 18:16

● ● ●

A multitude of other witnesses, when heard with an open mind and a correct *a priori* understanding of the location of the Temple and the location of Fort Antonia on the Haram gives new testimony to confirm the Biblical accounts.

Titus Flavius Josephus (previously cited) was a Jewish historian born in Jerusalem a few years after the death and resurrection of Jesus Christ. His writings from the late first century referenced Jesus, John the Baptist, and the spread of Christianity. He died around 100 CE, probably in his early sixties.

Although Josephus was born a Jew, he later became a Roman citizen. He was given access by the Romans to existing historical records that concerned the era of Roman control over Jerusalem and Palestine.

Josephus confirms the complete destruction of Jerusalem in 70 CE by his eyewitness account. He said *"Now the Romans set fire to the extreme parts of the city and burnt them down, and entirely demolished its [Jerusalem's] walls."*[40]

Note that the walls of Fortress Antonia were not damaged or burned down because they were not considered a part of Jerusalem, but rather, a Roman city- completely separate from Jerusalem. These walls are made of Herodian and pre-Herodian stones. For Jesus' prophecy to be true, they would have had to have been torn down, if, and only if they were a part of Jerusalem. But they were not. Fort Antonia survived the war and survives to this day.

---

[40] *War,* Volume 6, Chapter 9, Paragraph 4

Unfortunately, it has been mistakenly identified as the Temple Mount. One can only wonder what the Moslems would say if they ever were to realize that their holy site is built on an army camp.

Josephus also makes several interesting references that concern the Temple and Fortress Antonia.

"Now as to the Tower of Antonia, it might seem to be composed of several cities." If we compare this to the original twelve acres of the Jebusite city, or City of David, then that would be thirty-six acres.

Not only did he comment as to the size of Fortress Antonia, he also makes an observation as to its altitude. *"For if we go up to this Tower of Antonia, we gain the city since we shall then be upon the top of the hill."* Does this not describe the view of the city from the elevated 36-acre platform? Is this not why the golden Dome of the Rock dominates the skyline of Old Jerusalem?

In order to ensure the maintenance of law and order in Jerusalem, and specifically at the Temple site, Herod designed things to keep a close watch on the Temple as well as prepare for a quick response time in case of trouble. He did this through a pair of colonnades that connected the Fortress Antonia with the Temple. This is substantiated not only by Josephus, but by the Book of Acts:

And all the city was moved, and the people ran together: and they took Paul, and drew him out of the temple: and forthwith the doors were shut. And as they went about to kill him, tidings came unto the chief captain of the band, that all Jerusalem was in an uproar. Who immediately took soldiers and centurions, and ran down unto them: and when they saw the chief captain and the soldiers, they left beating of Paul.[41]

Note that:
1. Paul was in the temple
2. They drew him out of the temple, intending to kill him
3. The chief captain heard about what was going on
4. He immediately took soldiers and centurions…
5. And ran DOWN to them
6. They stopped the beating of Paul

The word *down* is key. If Paul had been on the so-called Temple Mount, there would be nowhere to run down from. Again, the Bible proves beyond the shadow of a doubt that Fortress Antonia was adjacent to and elevated above the Temple. Logic would confirm that the Romans would not build the massive Haram for the Jews and not place themselves in a position from which they could watch over it.

---

[41] *Acts 21:30-32*

Another witness comes from Masada. Masada was a fortress and retreat that Herod the Great had built for himself between 37 and 31 BCE. When the Romans began to persecute the Jews in the first century (CE), a group of them fled to the mountaintop refuge to escape the Romans.

They held out for three years after the fall of Jerusalem. The legendary siege ended when the Romans (stationed in a thirty-six acre camp at the base of Masada) built a ramp and invaded in the spring of 73 or 74 CE. When they breached the wall and entered the camp, they were surprised to find that 960 men, women, and children had committed mass suicide, rather than be captured by the Romans.

Eleazar Ben Ya'ir, a commander at Masada gave an eyewitness description of Jerusalem after the fall in 70 CE. He said "It [Jerusalem] is now demolished to the very foundations, and hath nothing left but that monument of it preserved, *I mean the camp of those (Romans) that hath destroyed it, which still dwells upon its ruins."*

This is clear and indisputable testimony that Fort Antonia, the Roman Camp was located on the one section of Jerusalem that was not considered a Jewish city, which was upon and above its ruins. Also, modern excavations of the rubble from this area have found fragments of latrines, something that would never have been allowed near the Temple.

In the third century, the historian Eusebius visited Jerusalem. He records "The hill called Zion and Jerusalem, the building there, that is to say, the temple, [has] been utterly removed or shaken."

One other visitor to the Holy City in 333 CE also notes the purpose for the great walled structure on the eastern side of Jerusalem. He is known only as the Bordeaux Pilgrim. His visit coincided with the building of the Church of the Holy Sepulcher. The Bordeaux Pilgrim visited the Church of the Holy Sepulcher, which is located west of the Haram. This visit would have been several centuries before the construction of the Dome of the Rock in 687 CE. The Bordeaux Pilgrim describes the walled structure with its foundational walls located in the bottom of the Tyropoeon (or Central) Valley, located to the west of the Mount.[42] He identifies it as the *Praetorium* where Pilate tried Jesus. The only walls visible looking east from the site of the Church of the Holy Sepulcher would have been the walls of the Haram, or Fortress Antonia.

There is also a silent witness, but this silent witness speaks volumes. Traditionally, historians believed that the final, outer layer of the retaining walls surrounding the Temple platform were built by Herod. Herod died in 4 BCE.

In 2011, while excavating under the Western Wall, archaeologists discovered a coin, minted some twenty years after the death of Herod. This ancient structure, which still stands today could not have been built in the time of Herod, nor could Herod's Temple have been built there.

---

[42] *The Temples that Jerusalem Forgot* by Ernest L Martin. ASK Publications, Portland, OR, 2000

• • •

It is likely this coin was dropped there somewhere between Jesus' second visit to the temple (age 12) and His final visit, around 29-30 CE. Again, this means that Herod did not complete the retaining walls of the so-called Temple Mount. They were not complete until sometime after Jesus' second visit to Jerusalem and the Temple, around 9 or 10 CE. Jesus' family visited the *Temple* when he was an infant. Jesus visited again at age twelve. The structure that is called the Temple Mount today was Fortress Antonia, and still under construction, and probably not completed until only a few years before his crucifixion and resurrection.

Chapter 8
The Jerusalem Jesus Knew

With these things in mind, we now have a good idea of the Jerusalem that Jesus knew. The Roman presence, established in 63 BCE grew under Herod and continued to grow into domination. Matthew 5:41, a revolutionary concept introduced by Jesus, teaches *"And whosoever shall compel thee to go a mile, go with him twain."* Here He is referring to Roman soldiers, who had the right to compel the Jews to carry their gear for a mile. Resentment was building on the part of the Jews, as well as their oppressors.

Geographically, Herod's Temple is located on the southeastern ridge of the city, where the original Mount Zion was truncated by the Hasmoneans in the Second Century, BCE. The Temple is separated from Fort Antonia by the raised area called the Ophel. Jerusalem has expanded to the west since the days of Nehemiah. There is now an upper city on the western side of the Central Valley, and the palace stands at its western edge. The city has grown on the northern side as well, but not as far west as the palace or the vicinity of the modern Joppa Gate.

● ● ●

The Mount of Olives is to the east of the city, across the Kidron Valley, where special olives are grown to make the oil for the light in the Temple. Directly across from the former location of the Temple in the City of David is a second, shorter mountain known today as Silwan. It has also been identified in older maps as the "Mount of Offense." Silwan is also the same root word as Siloam. The pool of Siloam (or "sent" John 9:7) was fed by the waters of the Gihon Spring, and was recently uncovered at the base of the City of David. It was used for purification by those who came to visit the Temple, further confirming its location in the City of David, directly above.

So Where Was Jesus Crucified?

We know that the crucifixion, death, burial, and resurrection of Jesus Christ took place in a relatively confined geographical area.

After this, Jesus knowing that all things were now accomplished, that the scripture might be fulfilled, saith, I thirst. Now there was set a vessel full of vinegar: and they filled a spunge with vinegar, and put it upon hyssop, and put it to his mouth. When Jesus therefore had received the vinegar, he said, It is finished: and he bowed his head, and gave up the ghost. The Jews therefore, because it was the preparation, that the bodies should not remain upon the cross on the sabbath day, (for that sabbath day was an high day,) besought Pilate that their legs might be

● ● ●

broken, and that they might be taken away. Then came the soldiers, and brake the legs of the first, and of the other which was crucified with him. But when they came to Jesus, and saw that he was dead already, they brake not his legs: But one of the soldiers with a spear pierced his side, and forthwith came there out blood and water. And he that saw it bare record, and his record is true: and he knoweth that he saith true, that ye might believe. For these things were done, that the scripture should be fulfilled, A bone of him shall not be broken. And again another scripture saith, They shall look on him whom they pierced. And after this Joseph of Arimathaea, being a disciple of Jesus, but secretly for fear of the Jews, besought Pilate that he might take away the body of Jesus: and Pilate gave him leave. He came therefore, and took the body of Jesus. And there came also Nicodemus, which at the first came to Jesus by night, and brought a mixture of myrrh and aloes, about an hundred pound weight. Then took they the body of Jesus, and wound it in linen clothes with the spices, as the manner of the Jews is to bury. Now in the place where he was crucified there was a garden; and in the garden a new sepulchre, wherein was never man yet laid. There laid they Jesus therefore because of the Jews' preparation day; for the sepulchre was nigh at hand.[43]

Note that *"the sepulchre was nigh at hand."* The stage for the greatest act of love and mercy in the history of the universe and reached every corner of time and space actually took place on a relatively small stage.

---

[43] John 19:28-42

But where was that stage? There are four main candidates placed in nomination for the place where Jesus Christ was crucified, buried, and arose victorious over death.

The Church of the Holy Sepulchre

The two silver domes upstaged by the massive gold dome of the Dome of the Rock to their east in the Old City of Jerusalem mark the location of the Church of the Holy Sepulcher in the Christian Quarter. Today, the Old City is divided into four quarters. The Christian Quarter is on the northwest, where the Church of the Holy Sepulcher is located. The Armenian Quarter is on the southwest, the Muslim Quarter is on the northeast, closest to the Haram/Temple Mount, and the Jewish Quarter on the southeast, near the City of David, and with access to the Western Wall, also called the "Wailing Wall." The Church of the Holy Sepulcher was completed in 335 CE. It was later destroyed in 1009 and subsequently rebuilt. The original building was directed by Constantine's mother, Helena. It is said that she had a great influence on her son. She was considered queen of the Roman Empire and has since been sainted by the Roman Catholic Church.

• • •

When Helena arrived in Jerusalem, it was still in a state of much devastation from the destruction in 70 CE. As mentioned earlier, the Bordeaux Pilgrim would identify some of the only walls standing as those of Fort Antonia. The Roman army had only been gone a few years earlier.

Hadrian had re-named the city Aelia Capitolina, in an attempt to rewrite history and purge it from its Jewish past.

When she was almost 80 years old (a ripe old age, especially in the fourth century) she made a pilgrimage to ancient Palestine with the hopes of locating the holy sites of the life of Jesus that had been neglected, and in some cases, all but lost. Helena arrived in Palestine around 327 CE. Apparently, work on the church began almost immediately. Helena died before its completion.

An interesting story survives as to how Helena determined that the former site of the Temple of Venus (which she removed) was supposedly the place where Christ was crucified and buried. In order to allegedly verify the location, she solicited the aid of Jews living in Jerusalem. One might only wonder about what latent feelings these Jews might have toward the Roman Empire, as well as the Emperor's mother. Finally, a man named Judas directed Helena where to dig, and three pristine crosses were unearthed, along with nails, a reed, a sponge, and the plaque nailed above the cross. Even more amazing is that these items had supposedly been buried for some three hundred years![44]

---

[44] *Golgotha: Searching for the True Location of Christ's Crucifixion* by Bob Cornuke. Koinonia House 2010

One good thing that the Church of the Holy Sepulcher does have in the "authenticity column" is that it indeed was outside the city walls in Jesus' time. It is inside the walls today, but remember that the walls have been moved and the city has been enlarged. However, the location, which is ***northwest*** of the Temple, added to the somewhat questionable means of determining its location.

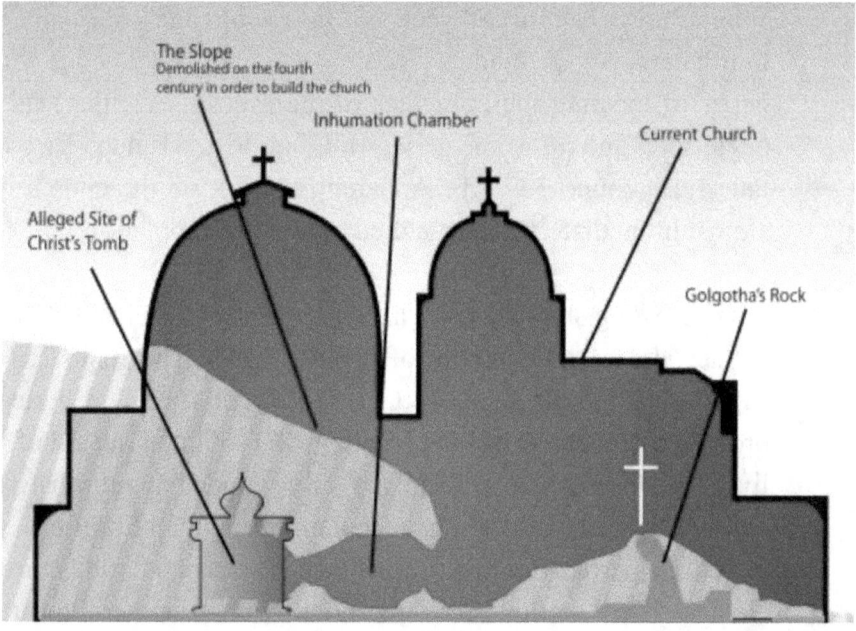

It is confusing and somewhat overwhelming to say the least. We toured the buildings twice. (Actually it is a complex of multiple buildings joined together.) The first time, we did not find the supposed location of Calvary. It is located at the top of a narrow staircase, where hostile monks alternate between scowls and naps as they sit in very uncomfortable looking chairs and carefully scrutinize and monitor spiritual pilgrims with suspicious glances.

* * *

In 1966, Michael Avi-Yonah created a 1:50 model of Jerusalem. Unfortunately, based on the information he had, and following traditional historical scholarship, he placed the Temple in the middle of what should be Fortress Antonia and not in the City of David. However, Avi-Yonah's model is an exquisite piece of work and is in many ways a great depiction of life in first-century Jerusalem.

The following picture is a scale re-creation of the small outcropping of rock in a quarry-like area *west* of the city. It is a representation of what those who believe that the Church of the Holy Sepulcher was actually the place where Jesus was crucified, buried and resurrected would have looked like in 29 BCE.

• • •

This is what it looks like today:

You really have to experience the Church of the Holy Sepulcher for yourself to understand what it is really like. Pictures show it to be a place of awe and majesty.

We also found it to be a place of strife and contention. Clerics sit in offices and scowl at other clerics and write decrees against them. It is difficult to fathom that the sour gentlemen pictured here works in this office literally only a few feet away from where he believes that the Lord Jesus Christ was crucified for his sins.

● ● ●

We were also stunned at the excessive ceremonialism and venerations of relics. This slab is supposedly the one used to prepare Jesus' body for burial. We saw many people put items on it and pray over it and even kiss it.

Only rare and slim beams of sunlight are allowed to permeate the inner recesses of this massive edifice. Prayers and masses are offered up constantly.

My personal observation when touring this place was that I was glad they called it the Church of the Holy Sepulcher, and not the Church of the Resurrection, because there is no spiritual life here. There are six different denominations that control what goes on in the Church of the Holy Sepulcher, and they fiercely compete to control exactly what goes on in their domain. In addition to the Roman Catholic Church (or Latin Church, as it is known in Israel), the Greek Orthodox, Armenian Apostolic, Coptic Orthodox, and Ethiopians Tewahedo all have some measure of control. And control is the theme.

• • •

One historical account that illustrates this is the Immovable Ladder, which can be seen below the upper window near the center of this picture. It seems that this ladder has been in the same place for some 250 years now, since there is a rule that no cleric can move or rearrange anything without the consent of the other five orders.[45]

It seems that There is no joy, no love, no grace, and no peace to be found here. Just a dead, empty tomb. Even if the historical evidence was compelling, one would have to ask if it were even possible if this were the place where Jesus was buried. There remains nothing of the spirit of His teachings.

---

[45] https://en.wikipedia.org/wiki/Immovable_Ladder

• • •

The Church of England (Anglicanism) has been in existence for about five hundred years. Protestantism was born in 1517. Both of these "new additions" to institutional Christianity did not come along until things were pretty well set in stone at the location of the Church of the Holy Sepulcher. After all, with six "Christian" Denominations already fighting for control, there really wasn't any more room at the table.

The Anglicans, Protestants, and even the Baptists needed a place to send their visitors to the Holy Land. And to be honest, they probably weren't overly welcome by the entrenched power brokers there or encouraged by their spiritual leaders back home to get too connected there. The second place, then, that we shall examine as to its claims to be the place where Jesus was crucified, buried, and resurrected is Gordon's Calvary and the Garden Tomb.

● ● ●

Gordon's Calvary and the Garden Tomb

The story of Gordon's Calvary and the Garden Tomb begin with a war hero, General Charles "Chinese" Gordon. His life was portrayed by Charlton Heston in the movie *Khartoum*.

When noted American Bible scholar, Edward Robinson

(later acclaimed as the "founder of Biblical Archaeology") visited Jerusalem in 1838, he began to sow the seeds of doubt as to the authenticity of the Church of the Holy Sepulcher as the genuine site of Christ's death, burial, and resurrection. While he did not propose an alternate site, others soon did. When Major General Gordon visited Jerusalem in 1882, the proverbial ball was already rolling, and Gordon's popularity and influence among the English speaking people shifted the balance of opinion to this new location, which has been come to be known as "Gordon's Calvary."

The Church of England (Anglicanism) has been in existence for about five hundred years. Protestantism was born in 1517. Both of these "new additions" to institutional Christianity did not come along until things were pretty well set in stone at the location of the Church of the Holy Sepulcher. After all, with six "Christian" Denominations already fighting for control, there really wasn't any more room at the table.

The Anglicans, Protestants, and even the Baptists needed a place to send their visitors to the Holy Land. And to be honest, they probably weren't overly welcome by the

• • •

entrenched power brokers there or encouraged by their spiritual leaders back home to get too connected there. The second place, then, that we shall examine as to its claims to be the place where Jesus was crucified, buried, and resurrected is Gordon's Calvary and the Garden Tomb.

The photo on the left was made around 1900. (Note the camels in the foreground.) The picture on the right was made in 2017. There is certainly room to assert that there is an appearance that could be called a skull in either photograph. The question that must be asked here is that if the stone on this mountain can change this much in one hundred years, how much could it have changed in 2000 years? It has even been reported that part of the nose fell off in 2015.[46]

[46] http://blog.bibleplaces.com/2015/03/nose-falls-off-skull-of-gordons-calvary.html

● ● ●

We know that Jesus was crucified in the "place of a skull."[47] But we know little, if anything as to *why* it was called the place of a skull. Did it look like a skull? Were there human skulls from previous executions? Was it just a name? We simply do not know.

It would also be worthwhile to observe that if Jesus had been crucified here, it would not have been on the top of the hill, but rather at the base. The desire of those administering the capital punishment would want those "passing by"[48] to see the end result of their victim's transgression. We also read the Biblical record of those who passed by Jesus cross:

"And they that passed by railed on him, wagging their heads, and saying, Ah, thou that destroyest the temple, and buildest it in three days,"[49]

It would be most unlikely that they would go out of their way to climb a small, but steep mountain just to pass by and revile Him. However, it is interesting to note that the ground at the base of the skull face is now a bus stop, and that the traditional location for Jeremiah's Grotto is in practically the same location.

However, not far from Gordon's Calvary, an unusual discovery was made.

---

[47] Matthew 27:33, Mark 15:22, John 19:17

[48] Lamentations 1:12

[49] Mark 15:29

The Garden Tomb

Unlike the Church of the Holy Sepulcher, the Garden Tomb is a peaceful, welcoming oasis amidst the chaos and bedlam of Jerusalem. Located north of the Damascus Gate, and only a few paces from Gordon's Calvary, it has provided believers and seekers alike a place of contemplation and peace.

The tomb was discovered, or actually, re-discovered in 1887, shortly after General Gordon's endorsement of Skull Hill. Everything seemed to be falling into place for the Anglicans and Protestants. However, this is the problem for all historians and archaeologists. We cannot try and use the Bible to justify our own opinions and whims. We must ask "What saith the Scriptures?"

Now in the place where he was crucified there was a garden; and in the garden a new sepulchre, wherein was

• • •

never man yet laid.[50]

The Garden Tomb (and Gordon's Calvary) certainly *looks* like what we would think Calvary and the real Tomb would look like. The tomb has a groove in front of it where it looks like a large stone would have rolled across the door.

And, behold, there was a great earthquake: for the angel of the Lord descended from heaven, and came and rolled back the stone from the door, and sat upon it.[51]

It is in a garden, evidenced by the discovery of an ancient olive press. The two are in close proximity to each other, and still outside the current walls of the city.

But just like the problem of the changes made by the years to the Skull, there is a problem with changes that *haven't* happened to the Garden Tomb. Recent archaeological discoveries, as well as the design of the Tomb indicate that it was much older than the time of Jesus or Joseph of Arimathea.[52] Additional studies on the groove that Gordon insisted must have been for the stone is more likely to be a trough for animals, built by the Crusaders.

Together, both the Skull and the Tomb are located *north* of the Temple. Although they were and still are outside the city walls, this must disqualify them from being authentic sites in the life of the Lord Jesus Christ.

---

[50] John 19:41   [51] Matthew 28:2
[52] https://en.wikipedia.org/wiki/The_Garden_Tomb

• • •

To their credit, the organization that operates the Tomb says on their website:

"Some may say as a result of visiting the Garden Tomb; 'I think I have found the place where Jesus died.' We hope and pray that they will find forgiveness through the death of Jesus and peace with God. Some may return home saying 'I saw the place where they put the dead body of Jesus.' It is far more important that they should discover the new life that Jesus offers now, and that they should share the next life with Him in heaven. Our staff will always be on hand to help our visitors, in a gentle and unobtrusive way, to answer their questions and to explain how they can discover these wonderful gifts of forgiveness and new life.[53]

We enjoyed our time at the Garden Tomb very much. The staff we crossed paths with were very sweet and hospitable. In many ways it is the opposite of the Church of the Holy Sepulcher. A stop there is a must for any spiritual pilgrim that visits Jerusalem. But realize that it is highly unlikely that it is the place where Jesus was crucified and buried.

Where Was Jesus Crucified?

Although we have seen where Jesus was *not* crucified, we are still back to our original question "Where was Jesus Crucified?" Let us consider what the Bible teaches.

---

[53] http://www.gardentomb.com/about/message-of-the-tomb/

And after this Joseph of Arimathaea, being a disciple of Jesus, but secretly for fear of the Jews, besought Pilate that he might take away the body of Jesus: and Pilate gave him leave. He came therefore, and took the body of Jesus. And there came also Nicodemus, which at the first came to Jesus by night, and brought a mixture of myrrh and aloes, about an hundred pound weight. Then took they the body of Jesus, and wound it in linen clothes with the spices, as the manner of the Jews is to bury. Now in the place where he was crucified there was a garden; and in the garden a new sepulchre, wherein was never man yet laid. There laid they Jesus therefore because of the Jews' preparation day; for the sepulchre was nigh at hand.[54]

Consider the following indisputable Scriptural facts:

1. Jesus was buried in a tomb owned by Joseph of Arimathea, a secret disciple, but apparently a man of some wealth and standing in the Jewish community.
2. Jesus' body was prepared for burial, but not altogether completed due to the encroaching Sabbath.
3. The preparation of Jesus' body involved winding it in linen clothes, in the custom of the Jews. There is no evidence of the Shroud of Turin in the Bible.

---

[54] John 19:38-42

• • •

4. There was a garden with a new sepulcher near the site of the Crucifixion. It is significant that the sepulcher had never been used. Jesus, as high priest could not touch a place where there had been a dead body.

5. To underscore and reiterate: Calvary and the Tomb were near each other. Apparently close enough to quickly transport a dead body without a large entourage, and to be able to do so in a short period of time.

These things we know and accept. But this passage alone does not give us sufficient information to decipher the information as to where the most transformational of all historical events took place. Let us consider Matthew's account of these events.

Jesus, when he had cried again with a loud voice, yielded up the ghost. And, behold, the veil of the temple was rent in twain from the top to the bottom; and the earth did quake, and the rocks rent; And the graves were opened; and many bodies of the saints which slept arose, And came out of the graves after his resurrection, and went into the holy city, and appeared unto many. Now when the centurion, and they that were with him, watching Jesus, saw the earthquake, and those things that were done, they feared greatly, saying, Truly this was the Son of God. And many women were there beholding afar off, which followed Jesus from Galilee, ministering unto him: Among which was Mary Magdalene, and Mary the mother of James and Joses, and the mother of Zebedee's children. When the even was come, there came a

• • •

rich man of Arimathaea, named Joseph, who also himself was Jesus' disciple: He went to Pilate, and begged the body of Jesus. Then Pilate commanded the body to be delivered. And when Joseph had taken the body, he wrapped it in a clean linen cloth, And laid it in his own new tomb, which he had hewn out in the rock: and he rolled a great stone to the door of the sepulchre, and departed. And there was Mary Magdalene, and the other Mary, sitting over against the sepulchre.[55]

Let us add to our list of indisputable facts from the indisputable Book. Several things happened at the moment Jesus died:

1. The veil in the temple was rent, or split in two. This veil was more than a thin piece of cloth, or even a thick curtain. Although the Bible does not specify the thickness, speculation runs from a handbreadth (four inches) to much more. The purpose of this veil, or barrier was to put a division between a Holy God and unholy humankind. It was split in two to show that there was no more division. There was no more need for a priesthood. Every man could approach God for himself.[56]

2. The veil was split in two *from top to bottom*. It is impossible for men could to have split the veil had he wanted to. One commentator says that a team of horses could not have torn the veil.

    Nevertheless, we are amazed that this act of

● ● ●

reconciliation and forgiveness toward humankind comes only from God. He is the initiator of the relationship we can have with Him.

3. There was an earthquake.

4. The rocks rent, like the veil. They split open.

5. The graves were opened.

6. Saints were resurrected, came out of the graves, and went into the city, and appeared to many people.

7. There was a centurion and a group of others with him. They saw:

   A. Jesus die.
   B. The earthquake
   C. And the other things that were done-specifically:
      - The rocks rent
      - The graves opened
      - The veil rent
8. They feared greatly and recognized that Jesus was the Son of God.

---

55 Matthew 27:50-61
56 Hebrews 4:16

In order to understand the true location of the Crucifixion of Jesus Christ, we must carefully examine every geographical clue given to us in the infallible Word of God. Notice carefully point 7 above. There is a colossal clue that we have failed to see for two millennia. Notice that one of the things that the centurion and his company *saw* that convinced them that Jesus was the Son of God was THE VEIL IN THE TEMPLE SPLIT IN TWO.

There is only one line of sight, one location anywhere near Jerusalem where anyone could SEE the veil in the Temple split or rent into two pieces.

That line of sight is not west of the Temple, where the Church of the Holy Sepulcher is located. Nor is it northwest of the Temple, where Gordon's Calvary and the Garden Tomb are located.

There was only one door in the Temple, as was in the Tabernacle. In both cases that door represented the doctrine of exclusivity:

Jesus saith unto him, I am the way, the truth, and the life: no man cometh unto the Father, but by me.[57]
*Then said Jesus unto them again, Verily, verily, I say unto you, **I am the door** of the sheep.*[58]

That door always faced east.

---

[57] John 14:6. See also Acts 4:12.
[58] John 10:7

But those that encamp before the tabernacle toward the east, even before the tabernacle of the congregation eastward, shall be Moses, and Aaron and his sons, keeping the charge of the sanctuary for the charge of the children of Israel; and the stranger that cometh nigh shall be put to death.[59]

The door of the Temple faced east. Even those who try to drag the Temple from the City of David and precariously balance it on the craggy mountain crest to the north still agree that THE TEMPLE DOOR FACED EAST. Again, it is crucial to understand that the only way the Centurion and his company could have seen the veil rent in two was from somewhere EAST of the Doors of the Temple.

---

[59] Numbers 3:38

Chapter 9
The Location of the Temple

We have already looked extensively at the subject of the true location of the temple. We have seen so many maps, models, and artists renditions of the Temple sitting on the Haram which was actually the Roman Fort Antonia that it is difficult for us to imagine it being in its original, correct location *south* of the modern-day platform.

The Red Heifer

And the Lord spake unto Moses and unto Aaron, saying, This is the ordinance of the law which the Lord hath commanded, saying, Speak unto the children of Israel, that they bring thee a red heifer without spot, wherein is no blemish, and upon which never came yoke: And ye shall give her unto Eleazar the priest, that he may bring her forth without the camp, and one shall slay her before his face: And Eleazar the priest shall take of her blood with his finger, and sprinkle of her blood directly before the tabernacle of the congregation seven times:[60]

• • •

There has been much ado about the recent birth of a Red Heifer in Israel. The Red Heifer was one of the sacrifices made by ancient Israel in the days of Temple sacrifices. It was a picture of the ultimate Sacrifice that would be made by Jesus Christ. It was not sacrificed at the door, or entrance to the Tabernacle or Temple, but it was led out by the priests to a specified distance away, outside the camp or the city walls. This is why it is so important to establish that Jesus was crucified outside the city walls. It was a sacrifice intended to purify those with leprosy, a type of sin in the Bible.

We have an altar, whereof they have no right to eat which serve the tabernacle. For the bodies of those beasts, whose blood is brought into the sanctuary by the high priest for sin, are burned without the camp. Wherefore Jesus also, that he might sanctify the people with his own blood, suffered without the gate. Let us go forth therefore unto him without the camp, bearing his reproach.[61]

During the days of Temple worship, the Red Heifer would be led out from the temple by the priests, crossing a bridge over the Kidron Valley, and sacrificed on the mountain on the other side of the valley.[62]

---

[60] Leviticus 19:1-4

[61] Hebrews 13:10-13

[62] http://www.jewishvirtuallibrary.org/red-heifer

● ● ●

Jesus fulfilled this when He was led out of the Temple by the priests, across the same bridge as the Red Heifer, and crucified on the same mountain, the same distance from the Temple, on the opposite side of the valley. The Via Dolorosa is as much a human creation as some of the stations on it. It just didn't happen that way.

From archaeology, then, we can find another clue that will help us pinpoint the true location of the Temple. If the temple was located on the Haram, where currently the Dome of the Rock sits, there would be some evidence of the existence of a bridge. The bridge would have gone across to the Mount of Olives, to the east.

There's only one problem with that: There is absolutely no archaeological evidence of a bridge having been there. None. Not even evidence of a bridge that was destroyed. No bridge.

But we know that the Red Heifer was led across a bridge. And the Lord Jesus Christ was led across that same bridge. But there is no evidence of a bridge going across from the *acclaimed* location of the temple to the opposite side of the Kidron Valley.

So where was the bridge that led to the place where they crucified Jesus? It was between the Temple in the City of David and the opposing hillside. You won't find something if you are looking for it in the wrong location.

Luke 23:33

* * *

And when they were come to the place, which is called Calvary, there they crucified him, and the malefactors, one on the right hand, and the other on the left.[63]

"There." If the Bible makes a big deal of the place, so should we. Not to turn it into a religious shrine, or to sell Jerusalem T-shirts and hats, but to remember what happened there.

"Were you THERE when they crucified my Lord?"

If the Jews haven't been able to keep up with the correct location of the Temple, it is no surprise that based on incorrect information, Christians have not kept up with the location of Calvary.

But we can plainly see that the two are connected. So where was Jesus crucified?

We know the Temple was located on the Ophel, south of the Temple Mount, on the former location of the threshing floor of Ornan the Jebusite in the City of David. We know exactly where that was.

---

[63] Luke 23:33

Looking west, across the Kidron Valley from the Mount of Olives to the south end of the Temple Mount and the Ophel. The modern, New City of Jerusalem is in the background.

Looking up from the Ophel to the El Aqsa Mosque located on the southwest corner of the Temple Mount.
So what's across from it?

Silwan Village

Silwan Village is a predominately Arab town located directly across the Kidron Valley from the City of David and the correct location of the Temple. It is overgrown with apartments and full of Arab people. Distrustful people, because they feel they have been mistreated by the Jews.

In ancient times, Silwan was a cemetery. It takes little speculation to assert that the local Necropolis could have also been a place of execution, and certainly would have been a good candidate to be known as "the place of the skull."

Recent demolition and construction in Silwan have uncovered some of those ancient tombs. However, the most amazing tombs in Silwan Village are not these, which simply prove that it was once a cemetery.

• • •

The next four pictures show Silwan Village in 1852, the 1870's, the 1880's, and in 1890.

1852   1870's

1880's   1890

In addition to the fact that Silwan Village began to grow and urbanize during these last 150 years or so another key detail becomes visible. A detailed analysis of the 1852 picture

• • •

reveals gaping holes, (which some have observed resemble the face of a skull) revealed by the absence of a rock face on the hillside directly across from the northern end of the City of David, where Herod's Temple would have stood in Jesus' day. Bob Cornuke, police detective turned Biblical Archaeologist informs us that geologists, archaeologists, and seismologists have concurred that this was the result of a *first-century earthquake*[64].

Cornuke has visited the treacherous Arab village, and has confirmed that many, if not most of these open graves are still visible behind the multitude of apartment buildings on the hillside across from the true location of the Temple.

---

[64] *Golgotha* by Robert Cornuke. Koinonia House, 2016

• • •

Today, the people of Silwan Village seem unaware of the historical impact their homes' and apartments' location has. They are just trying to survive in a changing world. Also, as Moslems, they believe that Jesus was only a mortal prophet, and not the Son of God. They believe his death was tragic, and do not believe in the resurrection. Another interesting set of facts about Silwan Village, or Silwan, as it is often referred to, is the name itself. The Arabic name Silwan, like many of the names of the Arabic villages and locations in Israel today, is a variation of the original Hebrew name. In the case of Silwan, the comparable Hebrew name is Siloam, as in the Biblical Pool of Siloam.

When he had thus spoken, he spat on the ground, and made clay of the spittle, and he anointed the eyes of the blind man with the clay, And said unto him, Go, wash in the pool of Siloam, (which is by interpretation, Sent.) He went his way therefore, and washed, and came seeing.[65]

The Biblical Pool of Siloam was a Jewish *mikveh*, or ritual pool or bath, used to cleanse one's self before visiting the temple. Here, the Bible gives us a translation of the Hebrew word *Siloam*. It means "sent."

The Pool of Siloam was built during Hezekiah's reign, between 718 and 686 BCE.[66] It was used from that time, throughout the Second Temple Period. It was fed by the Gihon Spring, and located south of the Temple.

---

[65] John 9:6-7

[66] https://en.wikipedia.org/wiki/Pool_of_Siloam

• • •

In the early 1900s, before Arab construction covered it up. Then, the location of the Pool of Siloam was lost until the Summer of 2004 when construction workers were digging around a drainage pipe. Some stone steps were uncovered, amazingly, about the time two archaeologists happened to pass by.

Today, this pool greatly helps define the location and the true Temple site. Realizing that those who washed in it would not have traveled all the way to the Haram to visit the Temple, but rather, the much shorter distance to the Temple on the Ophel, south of the Haram.

Here is this author, standing in the Pool of Siloam in 2017.

Another interesting historical factoid uncovered in my research is about the hill of Siloam (now the location of Siloam Village) in the 1800s. According to the next map, this southern extension of the Mount of Olives did have its own name before being known as Silwan. In this map from the late 1800s, it was known as the Mount of Offense.

Notice, also in the map, the Ophel, (below the incorrectly located Temple) and the Mount of Olives on the right. Below the Mount of Olives, across from the correct location of the Temple (in the City of David) is Silwan, labeled as the **Mount of Offense**. Perhaps this is because:

*Who was delivered for our **offences**, and was raised again for our justification.*[67]

What more appropriate place for that to occur than on the Mount of Offense! Whether the mount was named for the event or the event took place on the mount, either is a clue to its significance.

Of further note is the Valley of Hinnom and Aceldama to the immediate south.

And in those days Peter stood up in the midst of the disciples, and said, (the number of names together were about an hundred and twenty,) Men and brethren, this scripture must needs have been fulfilled, which the Holy Ghost by the mouth of David spake before concerning Judas, which was guide to them that took Jesus. For he was numbered with us, and had obtained part of this ministry. Now this man purchased a field with the reward of iniquity;

• • •

and falling headlong, he burst asunder in the midst, and all his bowels gushed out. And it was known unto all the dwellers at Jerusalem; insomuch as that field is called in their proper tongue, Aceldama, that is to say, The field of blood.[68]

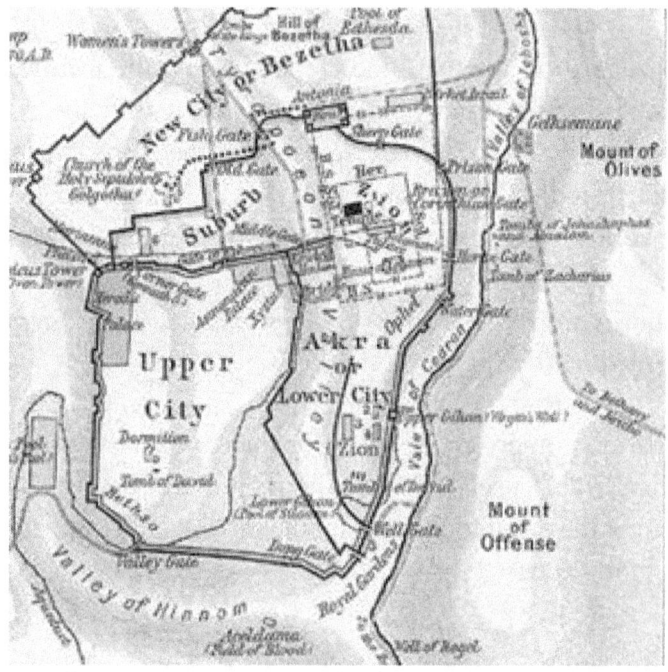

Notice also that the northern slope of the Mount of Offense is located due east of the Gihon Spring.

This is why there is no evidence to support the existence of this bridge in the location between the Haram and the Mount of Olives. It was between the actual Temple Mount and the Mount of Offense, or Silwan (where Jesus was Sent), where the view of the veil in the Temple was visible to the Centurion, and where the earthquake caused the

• • •

tombs to split open. Once again, you will not find something if you are looking in the wrong place. A place that had been used as a cemetery and a place of execution, likely known as the place of the skull. This is where Jesus Christ was crucified.

---

[67] Romans 4:25

[68] Acts 1:15-19

● ● ●

Artist's rendition of Calvary

Chapter 10
Where Was Jesus Resurrected?

Now in the place where he was crucified there was a garden; and in the garden a new sepulchre, wherein was never man yet laid. There laid they Jesus therefore because of the Jews' preparation day; for the sepulchre was nigh at hand.[69]

We do not know the exact location where the Cross stood that day. We can make a most reasonable assumption that it was east of the Temple, thus placing it somewhere in the Silwan Village. With the same degree of certainty, we can reasonably conjecture that the tomb was somewhere nearby. One interesting report comes from author Bob Cornuke in his book *Golgotha: Searching for the True Location of Christ's Crucifixion*. In chapter 14, Cornuke describes is recent visit to La Maison d'Abraham, a Catholic guest house. This property has a fenced garden that is adjacent to the Silwan Village. Tradition says that there is a cave where Jesus once taught the Disciples.

---

[69] John 19:41-42

* * *

The roof has caved in, but it also could have been an ideal and logical location for Jesus' burial and resurrection.

"Since before the early third century, when it is mentioned in the apocryphal Acts of John, one particular cave on the Mount of Olives has been regarded by Christians as the place where Jesus imparted this teaching to his inner group." [70]

Notice the word "before." It was in the third century that Helena, the mother of Constantine would come and miraculously discover Calvary and the tomb to the WEST of Jerusalem.

Perhaps future investigations will uncover more information about this site.

[70] John Wilkinson, PhD. *The Jerusalem Jesus Knew: An Archaeological Guide to the Gospels.*
(Nashville, TN: Thomas Nelson), 1978, page 119.

• • •

Chapter 11
First Century Jerusalem

After the death, burial, resurrection, and ascension of Jesus Christ, with the exception of the viral spread of Christianity, life continued in Jerusalem much as it had been for another generation. However, several Biblical incidents from the life of Paul as recorded in the New Testament give support to our position on the true location of the Temple, Calvary, and the Tomb. Because Christianity sprang from Judaism, and Jerusalem was essentially a Jewish City (despite the fact that it was under Roman occupation), the Temple was the center of Jewish life in the city. As a matter of fact, the Temple is mentioned more than two dozen times in the Book of Acts. There, the Christians assembled, taught, and prayed.

Of particular note in this early New Testament period is an account in Acts 21. It occurred around 60 C.E. Paul had returned to Jerusalem after his third missionary journey.

"Then Paul took the men, and the next day purifying himself with them entered into the temple, to signify the accomplishment of the days of purification, until that an

· · ·

offering should be offered for every one of them. And when the seven days were almost ended, the Jews which were of Asia, when they saw him in the temple, stirred up all the people, and laid hands on him, Crying out, Men of Israel, help: This is the man, that teacheth all men every where against the people, and the law, and this place: and further brought Greeks also into the temple, and hath polluted this holy place. (For they had seen before with him in the city Trophimus an Ephesian, whom they supposed that Paul had brought into the temple.) And all the city was moved, and the people ran together: and they took Paul, and drew him out of the temple: and forthwith the doors were shut. And as they went about to kill him, tidings came unto the chief captain of the band, that all Jerusalem was in an uproar. Who immediately took soldiers and centurions, and ran down unto them: and when they saw the chief captain and the soldiers, they left beating of Paul. Then the chief captain came near, and took him, and commanded him to be bound with two chains; and demanded who he was, and what he had done. "[71]

Notice here several statements of fact:

1. Paul's presence in the Temple caused an uproar.

2. Because of the uproar, the people were about to kill him.

3. They drew him out of the Temple and closed the doors.

4. The "chief captain of the band" took soldiers and centurions. This obviously points to the chief captain of the Roman tenth legion, stationed in Jerusalem at Fortress Antonia, which was positioned in order to keep an eye on the Temple and its surroundings.

5. The "chief captain of the band" took soldiers and centurions. This obviously points to the chief captain of

• • •

the Roman tenth legion, stationed in Jerusalem at Fortress Antonia, which was positioned in order to keep an eye on the Temple and its surroundings.

6. They *"ran down unto them…"* The immediate appearance of the Romans caused them to stop beating Paul, who was taken into Roman custody.

The key fact to determining the placement of Fortress Antonia and the Temple is that the soldiers and centurions "ran down." The highest place in Jerusalem that could have accommodated a significant number of Roman military would have been what is now known as the "Temple Mount," which was actually Fortress Antonia, as we have already discussed. Had the Temple been located on the "Temple Mount," they would have had to 'run UP' to them. Fortress Antonia was strategically positioned on the massive Haram or "Temple Mount" in order to have a good view and quick access to the area around the Temple just for instances like this one.

---

71 Acts 21:26-33

● ● ●

Haram/ "Temple Mount"/ Fortress Antonia on far right. Temple would have been in area on left.

Would they have had to "run down"? Obviously, yes.

Another street-level view from the southeast looking toward the Al-Aqsa Mosque on the Haram. Up or Down? They ran **down**, right through this area. Some say the Roman camp may have even extended into this area.[72]

Another piece of the puzzle materializes two chapters later, in Acts 23:

"And he called unto him two centurions, saying, Make ready two hundred soldiers to go to Caesarea, and horsemen threescore and ten, and spearmen two hundred, at the third hour of the night..."[73]

---

[72] *The Complete Guide to the Temple Mount Excavations.* Mazat, Eilat
[73] Acts 23:23

The thing to notice here is that two hundred soldiers, seventy horsemen (and presumably horses) along with two hundred more spearmen were dispatched to take Paul to Caesarea (some 75 miles to the northwest, on the Mediterranean), where he could appeal to Caesar. Paul was escorted by 470 Roman soldiers, plus Centurions. Apparently, this did not deplete the number of soldiers in Jerusalem to the point of creating a problem keeping a volatile city securely under Roman control.

The historical location on the Mediterranean where Paul was taken to appeal to Caesar

A Word on Avi-Yonah's Model

The Israel Museum in Jerusalem currently houses a 1:50 scale model of Jerusalem in the late Second Temple period. It was meticulously created by Michael Avi-Yonah, based on the best knowledge of his day.[74] The model depicts Fortress Antonia as an appendage to the Haram or "Temple Mount." Unfortunately several major inaccuracies have materialized in this depiction.

Photo of Avi-Yonah's 1:50 model. Note his depiction of Fortress Antonia appended on to the Temple on the back right corner of the Temple walls. The Jews would have never tolerated this. First, the Tenth Roman Legion and their support personnel (approximately 10,000 people) could not possibly have fit inside such a small structure.

---

[74]https://en.wikipedia.org/wiki/Holyland_Model_of_Jerusalem

• • •

Secondly, there has never been a shred of historical or archaeological evidence uncovered to support its existence in this location.

70 CE

Most scholars place Paul's death around 66 or 67 CE. By this time, things were heating up in Jerusalem. A group of devout Jews had taken Herod's former mountaintop resort near the Dead Sea, called Masada.

In one of the most tragic stories ever told, when the Romans finally penetrated the fortress by building a ramp up the side of the 300 foot near-vertical cliffs on the eastern side, they found some 960 Jewish men, women, and children had committed mass suicide rather than be conquered by the Romans.

However, some amazing historical facts survived the inhabitants of Masada, as well as their historical testimony of the total destruction of Jerusalem, save for the habitation of the Romans who destroyed it. This is an obvious reference to the still-undestroyed Haram which once overlooked the city and the former location of the Temple to the south.

In 284 CE, the Roman Tenth Legion finally deserted Jerusalem and apparently abandoned their long-time encampment there. A scant forty-two years later, Helena arrived to begin her supervision of the construction of the Church of the Holy Sepulcher in 326. Although she was reported to have died in 330[75], the work went on.

* * *

Again, we must remember that a few years after her death, the pilgrim from the Bordeaux region of France came for a visit to the Holy City. He described Jerusalem, as it appeared in 333 CE. His account is enlightening.

He arrived at the Church of the Holy Sepulcher, which was still in the process of being built. His account and description from that site, while looking eastward is quite noteworthy. He described stone walls with foundations extending downward into the Tyropoean valley. This valley is located immediately west of the Haram. In other words, he was obviously looking at the walls of the Haram, or so-called "Temple Mount." He describes these walls as the praetorium of the Romans. Apparently, the praetorium was still identifiable. This location is mentioned in the Bible.

*"And so Pilate, willing to content the people, released Barabbas unto them, and delivered Jesus, when he had scourged him, to be crucified. And the soldiers led him away into the hall, called **Praetorium**; and they call together the whole band. And they clothed him with purple, and platted a crown of thorns, and put it about his head, And began to salute him, Hail, King of the Jews! And they smote him on the head with a reed, and did spit upon him, and bowing their knees worshipped him. And when they had mocked him, they took off the purple from him, and put his own clothes on him, and led him out to crucify him."[76]*

[75] https://en.wikipedia.org/wiki/Helena_(empress)
[76] Mark 15:15-20

• • •

According to the Bordeaux Pilgrim, the first recorded Christian pilgrim to the Holy Land, the Haram and modern-day Dome of the Rock were not the location of the Temple, but rather the place where the Lord Jesus Christ was beaten, mocked, scourged, and led away to be Crucified.[77]

Aerial view of Masada.

---

[77] Cornuke, Bob *Temple* p. 54-55

• • •

Chapter 12
A New Force in the Middle East

It seems that the centuries in the Ancient Middle East could drag by at an astonishingly slow pace. What seems to have been a relevant flurry of activity in the late third and early fourth centuries yielded to more than two centuries of waiting and routine political shifting.

In 570 CE, everything changed. Muhammad ibn 'Abdullah was born in Mecca, in modern-day Saudi Arabia.[78] He would become the founder of a new worldwide religion, Islam. His early years were spent as a merchant. Somewhere about the time of his fortieth birthday, he became a religious leader. He united the peoples of the Arabian Peninsula behind his monotheistic teachings and Islam was born. Although he died at the age of 62, his teachings lived on and have continued to gain popularity.[79]

---

[78] Karsh, Efraim, *Islamic Imperialism a History,* p. 10-13
[79] https://en.wikipedia.org/wiki/Muhammad

Places of significance in Muhammad's life intertwined with oral tradition to evolve in to the holy sites of the new religion.

Back to the Temple Mount

In 621, Muhammad, on his faithful steed Buraq, is reported to have departed from the pinnacle of the Haram in Jerusalem for a fantastic journey. The faithful say Muhammad's footprints and Buraq's hoofprints are still visible in the rock there to this day. To commemorate what was to become the third holiest site in Islam (after Mecca and Medina), the Dome of the Rock was constructed in 687, on what was formerly the location of a pagan Roman temple.[80] (Historically, the gold on the dome was added by the King of Jordan in 1959.)

[80] https://en.wikipedia.org/wiki/Dome_of_the_Rock

Fast forward a few centuries. The pope had authorized the Crusades to take back the Holy Land. So, in 1099, the Crusaders replaced the crescent moon on top of the dome with a cross and renamed it "The Lord's Temple" or in Latin, "Templum Domini." Soon thereafter, the Knights Templar (or 'Knights of the Temple') took up residence on the presumed "Temple Mount." In 1167, Saladin reclaimed Jerusalem for the Muslims and restored the crescent moon to the Dome of the Rock. So, it would remain for many centuries, while historians recalled the days before Saladin's restoration as the days of "The Lord's Temple" and its location as "The Temple Mount."

Historians and archaeologists in the Holy Land will tell you that we are uncertain on some ancient sites, somewhat certain on others, and relatively certain on a few. But the one site they unanimously agree that we got right is that the Temple of Solomon and the Second Temple were located on the "Temple Mount."

It is difficult to admit you were wrong. And the longer you perpetuate the big lie, the more difficult it becomes to admit it. You become deceived yourself.

Chapter 13
The Dawn of a New Era

On May 2, 1860, Theodore Herzl was born[81]. He is credited with being the founder of Zionism[82], or the effort to establish (or reestablish) a homeland for the Jewish people in Israel in the Twentieth Century.

Jerusalem and its surrounding territories (Israel) had been conquered by the Ottoman Empire in 1516, and remained in Ottoman (Turkish) control until the British conquered Turkey in World War I. Then, on November 2, 1917, Arthur Balfour, a member of the British Conservative Party and former Prime Minister of the United Kingdom issued the Balfour Declaration, which expressed the view that Israel should have a homeland in what was then known as Palestine.[83] This put the wheels in motion for the establishment of the Jewish State (shortly after World War II) on May 14, 1948.

---

[81] https://en.wikipedia.org/wiki/Theodor_Herzl
[82] https://en.wikipedia.org/wiki/Zionism
[83] https://en.wikipedia.org/wiki/Balfour_Declaration

• • •

Interestingly, during this same time period from the early days of Zionism another discovery was made. In 1867, another Englishman, this time an engineer, Sir Charles Warren discovered a water shaft (gutter, waterspout, conduit) running from the water spring below up to the City of David[84]. Accounting for a major earthquake in 1067, it is likely that this is the shaft by which David conquered the Jebusite city some 2900 years before. It also proves that there was indeed running water in the Temple.

The Future Temple

The implications to Bible Prophecy and Eschatology are staggering. From the Book of Daniel, Chapter 9, we know that the Antichrist will defile the Temple during the seven-year Tribulation. However, this Temple has yet to be build. The Muslims, who are in control of the "Temple Mount" have stated that if any Jew as much as turns over one shovel of dirt, World War III will erupt as millions of Muslims come to defend the Dome of the Rock.

What if the Jews discover instead that the Jewish Temple never was on the "Temple Mount" but was instead south of the Temple Mount in the City of David. Remember here that God specifically told David to purchase the threshing floor from Ornan.

---

[84] https://en.wikipedia.org/wiki/Warren%27s_Shaft

• • •

"Then David said to Ornan, Grant me the place of this threshingfloor, that I may build an altar therein unto the Lord: thou shalt grant it me for the full price: that the plague may be stayed from the people. And Ornan said unto David, Take it to thee, and let my lord the king do that which is good in his eyes: lo, I give thee the oxen also for burnt offerings, and the threshing instruments for wood, and the wheat for the meat offering; I give it all. And king David said to Ornan, Nay; but I will verily buy it for the full price: for I will not take that which is thine for the Lord, nor offer burnt offerings without cost. So David gave to Ornan for the place six hundred shekels of gold by weight. And David built there an altar unto the Lord, and offered burnt offerings and peace offerings, and called upon the Lord; and he answered him from heaven by fire upon the altar of burnt offering."[85]

Israel owns the title deed to the original location of the Temple, in the City of David, over the Gihon Springs, on the Threshing floor of Ornan the Jebusite, purchased by King David himself. The Temple can be rebuilt there any time the Jewish people so desire.

It is also common knowledge that the Temple Institute in Jerusalem has recreated the various furnishings and vessels for the coming Temple[86]. Some of them are currently on display there.

---

[85] 1 Chronicles 21:22-26

[86] https://free.messianicbible.com/feature/the-temple-vessels-are-ready-for-the-rebuilding-of- jerusalems-third-temple/

The Millennial Temple

Like Zerubbabel's Temple, defiled by Antiochus Epiphanes, after the Tribulation Temple has been defiled by the Antichrist, yet another Temple will be built. This Temple is spoken of by Isaiah, Ezekiel, Daniel, Haggai, and Zechariah[87]. Specifically, Ezekiel foresees water flowing out of the Millennial Temple.

"Afterward he brought me again unto the door of the house; and, behold, waters issued out from under the threshold of the house eastward: for the forefront of the house stood toward the east, and the waters came down from under from the right side of the house, at the south side of the altar. Then brought he me out of the way of the gate northward, and led me about the way without unto the utter gate by the way that looketh eastward; and, behold, there ran out waters on the right side."[88]

---

[87] Isaiah 2:3, 56:6-7, 60:13, Ezekiel 40:1-47:1-2, Daniel 9:24, Joel 3:18, Haggai 2:7-9, Zechariah 6:12-15, 8:20-23.

[88] Ezekiel 47:1-2

Conclusion

Wherever Jesus was crucified, buried, and resurrected was not likely to have been either of the existing places that are observed or venerated as such today. Historically and archaeologically speaking, the tomb of Jesus was largely ignored by His followers, as it was only borrowed from a member of the Sanhedrin. Historically, it was probably destroyed by Hadrian sometime after135.[89]

Other solid rock tombs, with rolling stone doors, which have been uncovered by more recent archaeological digs. This type of tomb would also be typical of those that would be used by wealthy families.

The city of Jerusalem has changed constantly and radically over the last two thousand years. Our knowledge of the specific geographic locations of the events of Jesus' life and death is limited to general knowledge. No one today knows for certain exactly where His death, burial, and resurrection took place. Those who follow traditional scholarship are profoundly mistaken and confused.

---

[89] 2002 Hugh Claycombe, published by Rose Publishing, Inc

• • •

Perhaps this is by Divine design. Perhaps it was God's plan that we seek and worship the Saviour Who died for our sins, was buried, and arose victorious, rather than the exact place where it happened. The most important question is not *where* it happened, but *that* it happened, and that it is real to you as a personal reality.

It is possible that continued Biblical scholarship, archaeology, and the fulfillment of Prophecy will show us in the days and years to come. Hopefully, tradition will lose its hold on the minds of those who most ardently seek the truth. It may yet be possible to stand there and remember the Saviour Who died there and Who rose again from that very spot.

ABOUT THE AUTHOR

David B. Carpenter is a native of Mobile, Alabama. He and his wife are the parents three grown children. He has worked as a pastor, assistant pastor, and Christian school principal. He has also been instrumental in the founding of a radio station and hosted a weekly video webcast while in the St. Louis Area.

After being involved with full-time ministry for 30 years, David was introduced to a unique business opportunity protecting families and small businesses in 2009.

As a full-time entrepreneur, David enjoys traveling, speaking, collecting vintage microphones, and helping people achieve their personal and financial dreams. He is also a John C. Maxwell Certified Speaker, Trainer, and Coach.

WHAT IS UPSPYRE?

Upspyre was founded to give. Our founder, David B. Carpenter has been blessed to receive in life. He was raised in a wonderful home, and has been happily married for many years. He understands the importance of giving back.

● ● ●

David believes that our work is what we do to maintain our obligations and our lifestyle. Our ministry is what we do to give back. This is how we change the world.

WHAT OTHERS ARE SAYING

If I were asked to describe David Carpenter I would say he is a genuinely kind individual who is sincerely interested in the well-being of others. He is a dynamic motivational speaker who inspires his audiences. Upspyre, his company, was created to help families, businesses and churches. Teaching through talking is a gift that he utilizes to create those "ah-ha" moments for his listeners.

-Charlsie Pecoraro, Collective Minds, MeetDaBoss.com

I have known David Carpenter for many years, and I can say without any hesitation that David is an outstanding individual, with integrity, compassion and one of the most genuine attitudes in leadership that I have ever met. If you have David on your side, you are not going to lose. David is a great professional speaker and an awesome leadership counselor. I had David conduct a leadership training for my office staff a few months back and I can see much improvement with my staff making independent decisions and going above and beyond their job duties. I give David kudos for helping my staff get to the next level.

-Gina Germany, Touching Hearts Senior Care, Gulf Coast Dementia Services

I have brought in Mr. David Carpenter on countless occasions to speak to our staff, subcontractors, customers, and prospective customers. I have consistently relied on the professionalism and impactful teaching and speaking he has provided for my companies for many years. He has proven to be a dynamic, engaging, and authentic presenter and trainer every time he has come in.

-Kevin Mohler, Founder of StrategicLifeDesign.com

• • •

BIBLIOGRAPHY

Backhouse, Robert *The Kregel Pictorial Guide to the Temple* Grand Rapids: Kregel 1996 Bauer, Conrad *The Knights Templar* Maplewood Publishing

Ben-Abba, Dov *Israeli Album* New York: Harry N. Abrams, Inc. 1967

Cornuke, Robert *Golgotha* Cour d'Alene: Koinonia House 2016

Cornuke, Robert *Temple* Charlotte: Life Bridge 2014

Dehoney, Wayne *An Evangelical's Guide to the Holy Land* Nashville: Broadman Press 1974 deWohl, Louis *Saint Helena and the True Cross* New York: Farrar, Stratus and Cudahy 1958 Doyle, Stephen C. *The Pilgrim's New Guide to the Holy Land* Collegeville: Liturgical Press 1999

Edersheim, Alfred *The Temple and Its Ministry and Services* Peabody: Hendrickson Publishers 1994

● ● ●

Finkelstein, Israel *The Bible
Unearthed* New York: Free Press
2001 Gardner, Joseph L. *Atlas of
the Bible* Readers Digest 1981

Josephus, Flavius *The Complete Works of Flavius
Josephus* Grand Rapids: Kregel. 1981 Karsh, Efraim
Islamic Imperialism New Haven: Yale University Press
2007

Keller, W. Phillip *David the Shepherd
King* Waco: Word Books 1986 Kent,
Charles F. *Biblical Geography and
History* Ottawa: Petra Books 1911

Kollek, Teddy *Jerusalem* Jerusalem:
Steimatzky 1968

Levy, David M. *The Tabernacle: Shades of the
Messhiah* Bellmawr: Friends of Israel 2003

Lieberman, Saul *Greek in Jewish Palestine* New
York: Philipp Feldheim Inc. 1965 Lockyer, Herbert
All the Men of the Bible Grand Rapids: Zondervan

● ● ●

1968

Martin, Ernest L. *Secrets of Golgotha* Portland:

Associates for Scriptural Knowledge 1996 Martin,

Ernest L. *The Temples That Jerusalem Forgot*

Portland: ASK Publications 2000 Montefiore, Simon S.

Jerusalem the Biography New York: Random House

2011 Morton, H.V. *In Search of the Holy Land* New

York: Dodd, Mead & Company 1979 Pfeiffer, Charles

F. *Baker's Bible Atlas* Grand Rapids: Baker Book

House 1961

Pfeiffer, Ida *A Visit to the Holy Land,*

Egypt, and Italy Public Domain Price,

Randall *Rose Guide to the Temple*

Peabody: Rose Publishing 2012

Pritchard, James *Atlas of the Bible*

Ann Arbor: Borders Press 2003

Provan, Iain *A Biblical History of Israel* Louisville:

Westminster John Knox Press 2015 Reicke, Bo *The New*

• • •

Testament Era Philadelphia: Fortress Press. 2001

Rhodes, Ron *The 10 Things You Need to Know about*

Islam Eugene: Harvest House 2007 Rice, John R.

Here We Are In Bible Lands Murfreesboro: Sword of

the Lord 1977 Ruckman, Peter S. *The Tabernacle*

Pensacola: Bible Baptist Bookstore 1985

Soltau, Henry W. *The Tabernacle, The Priesthood, and the*

Offerings Grand Rapids: Kregel Publishers 1983

Sproul, R. C. *The Dark Side of Islam* Wheaton: Crossway
Books 2003

Teringo, J. Robert *The Land & People Jesus Knew*

Minneapolis: Bethany House 1985 Uncredited *Then and*

Now Bible Maps Rose Publishing

Ward, Kaari *Jesus and His Times* Readers Digest 1987

Warren, Charles *The Recovery of Jerusalem* New York:

D. Appleton & Company 1871 Wilkinson, John *The*

Jerusalem Jesus Knew Nashville: Thomas Nelson. 1978

Wright, G. Ernest *Great People of the Bible and How They*

Lived Pleasantville: Readers Digest 1974

● ● ●

PHOTO CREDITS

Pg. 19: www.youtube.com/watch?v=zKqDx3RDCos

Pg. 26: en.wikipedia.org/wiki/Solomon%27s_Temple

Pg. 35: ixora.pro/hezekiah-s-tunnel-jerusalem-map/hezekiah-s-tunnel-discovery

Pg. 36: www.youtube.com/watch?v=zKqDx3RDCos

Pg.41: pastormtzionbaptistblog.blogspot.com/2011/05/temple-comparison.html

Pg. 43: mtbiblestudies.com/clndrdte_My20,21_more.htm

Pg. 49: www.ancient.eu/image/336/the-empire-of-alexander-the-great/

Pg. 55: www.youtube.com/watch?v=ExEKO0cMtNU

Pg. 58: israel-tourguide.info/

Pg. 62: Reuters.com

Pg. 66: www.bibleplaces.com/holysepulcher/

Pg. 70: en.wikipedia.org/wiki/Destruction_of_the_Church_of_the_Holy_Sepulchre

Pg. 77: Left photo: Wikipedia.org / Right photo: Author

Pg. 100: Top: Wikipedia

Pg. 101: Golgotha by Robert Cornuke

Pg. 104: www. commons.wikimedia.org

Pg. 114: Wikipedia

Pg. 116: en.wikipedia.org/wiki/First_Crusade

• • •